QUEEN
with a
Pure White Crown

The adventuresome biography of

Mary M. Haas,

the Story-Teller
who charmed her audiences
wherever she went.

by her friend,

Ruth M. Jacobson

Typeset in the USA by
International Graphics
P.O. Box 38006   Charlotte, NC 28273

Printed in Canada by
Essence Publishing
44 Moira St., West, Belleville, ON   K8P1S3

This book is lovingly dedicated
to the families of

Mary M. Haas

and

Ruth M. Jacobson

To God be all the Glory!

Contents

Nigeria,

the most highly-populated country in West Africa.
The Lord is building His church there for His glory.

Kwoi is west of Jos in Plateau State.
Kurmin Musa is 14 miles south of Kwoi.
Rinjin Gani is 23 miles east of Jos in Bauchi State.

Introduction

"**By Popular Request**" was one of the many titles considered for this book. The contents are a modest attempt to tell the story and the stories of Mary M. Haas. Through many years of winsomely relating her unusual experiences in Africa, friends and audiences have urged Mary to preserve them in book form as a permanent record of God's faithfulness. Providence placed me in a retirement apartment close to Mary's abode. She asked me to do the honors. I am grateful for the privilege. I am also very much aware of the need for God's blessing on the readers so that the impact of Mary's life may bring a sweet consciousness of His pervasive grace and power, operative in His handmaiden's character and ministry.

There is a sadly-prevalent recognition that missionary books "do not sell, so why publish them?" The record of Mary Haas' exciting life seems to warrant attention as an inspiration and a challenge to all who would follow Christ on the journey from youth to old age. The author harbors more than wishful thinking that Mary's story may dispel the notion that missionary books fail to win and hold the interest of readers. Much of the story, market-tested on my own grandchildren, would fill a need when a child says, "Mommy or Daddy, will you read to me, please?"

The title reflects Mary's name in the Hausa language of Nigeria, a language familiar to those of many tribes who also have their own vernaculars. Though Mary initially learned the Jaba language of northern Nigeria, most of her people knew Hausa as well. It was the lingo of the marketplace. In her last twenty years in Nigeria she used Hausa, and thus the name Queen, *Sarauniya*, was affixed to this stately missionary. The Bible says that "The hoary head is a crown of glory." Mary's hair is as white as hoar frost, and frequently sets her off, even in a crowd. It turned white while she was quite young, much to her advantage. White hair is greatly respected in Africa where the average life-span is much shorter than in the West.

Mary now has the distinction of being one of the two oldest living SIM missionaries. There are about 1,900 of us! Could any one be loved more dearly by Nigerians, mission administrators, fellow-workers, donors, intercessors, and members of the churches and other agencies into which she poured her devotion to Christ?

The full roll-call of all S.I.M.missionaries in 1925 was not long. In fact, when a recruiter at Moody Bible Institute was pleading for workers for S.I.M., he was seeking to reach the goal of total membership of 100. Mary's name was added that year when she was not quite 24 years old. In those days the name, S.I.M., meant "Sudan Interior Mission." The "Sudan" was the geographical term covering the countries south of the Sahara Desert, stretching from the west coast to the east coast of Africa — "The land of the blacks." Later, the name, "Anglo-Egyptian Sudan," was affixed to an East Africa country under Britain's control. Upon independence it became simply, "The Sudan," hence the mission name became confusing to those who thought that our work must be limited to that section of East Africa, whereas the preponderance of our efforts were in Ethiopia and in West Africa. All of our overseas work in those days was on the continent of Africa, with headquarters in Canada, the U.S.A., the U.K., Australia, and New Zealand.

The S.I.M. has undergone changes and enlargements of its scope of ministry. Some years ago the Andes Evangelical Mission of South America became an integral part of the S.I.M., as did also the International Christian Fellowship of East Asia. Thus, the diverse overseas ministries quickly embraced about 37 countries in North and South America, Africa, and Asia. The name of the mission had to be changed, though the familiarity with the initials was too important to forfeit. The same initials were retained with a new denotation, **Society for International Ministries**. Adding to the diversity of challenges facing the mission, the influx of large numbers of internationals within the borders of the multiplied SIM home-base countries brought the opportune and rewarding impetus of ministry to our foreign guests and immigrants—"Ethnic Focus."

The vision and the scope of the work have greatly increased with the years. Thousands of self-governing, self-supporting, and self-propagating churches have emerged as SIM personnel have loved, taught, preached, and healed in Christ's name. The motto and the driving force of SIM remains the same. Its motto declares:

The Purpose of SIM is to Glorify God

by planting, strengthening and partnering with churches around the world as we:

*evangelize the unreached
*minister to human need
*disciple believers into churches
*equip churches to fulfill Christ's commission.

During Mary Haas' 72 years of membership in SIM, she has exemplified that motto as well as any human channel of God's power could do. As her friend, co-worker, and neighbor, I invite you to share in the blessings of her life as recorded in this little book. It is written for the glory of God and for the enjoyment of His beloved people. *"Allah ya sa albarka,"* as the Hausa people would say upon completing any task — "May God put His blessing upon it."

—Ruth M. Jacobson, 4109 Nigeria Rd., Sebring, Florida 33872

Information about SIM may be obtained from
SIM/USA, Box 7900, Charlotte, NC 28241
Phone: (704) 588-4300; FAX; (704) 587-1518

1

Not a Stork, but a Balky Horse

Who hasn't seen a four-year-old pull a temper-tantrum? It may be a common sight, but seldom has a balky horse been vociferously blamed for such antics. Seldom, but it did happen.

Mary Minnie Haas was born on the last day of 1901 to Jacob and Sarah Haas of Pandora, Ohio. Jacob was a lay preacher, a farmer, a loving husband and the father of eight children. The youngsters enjoyed a very happy childhood. They were far from being wealthy, but were richly surrounded by the parents' and grandparents' love. The family survived on the fruits of their land and their joint labor. They participated with neighbors in child-births, hog-slaughters, and every other challenge that drew rural people together. Those were good days.

Jacob wisely provided his five boys with a jointly-owned bicycle, and his three girls with a bike that they, too, could call their own. Those bikes loom large in memories of fraternal learning sessions, crashes and flops, uproarious races, errands, and appetite-arousing exercise. The blades of the family sled cut many a glistening swath through the newly-fallen winter snow as eight hefties tested the pulling stamina of the family's trusty bull. The boys had trained him to bear their total weight as he lumbered along, impressing upon the snow a confused pattern of hoofs and blades. If he groaned under the burden, the kids' shouts of glee muffled any bullish attempt to elicit sympathy.

Amidst all the clean fun, family closeness, and spiritual cohesiveness, Mary had a problem, enigmatic to any one who knows her today. She and one brother, two years older than she, both had tempers that could flare up quite easily. One day four-year-old Mary made a classic display of her fury. She swaggered through the kitchen and out to the path leading to the road. Then abruptly she turned around to declare her avowed intentions to her mother and oldest sister, Clara. "I'm going to run away!" Her mother ran out and said, "Wait a minute! I'll pack your clothes!" Clara and Mama, as they called her, quickly grabbed a gunny sack, stuffed it full of rags, and handed it to Mary.

Mary's resolve melted, and the rags missed their chance to be donned in some faraway haven of revenge.

Any one who knows Mary well smells sauerkraut cooking in her apartment fairly often. Making sauerkraut was a Haas family tradition, involving a huge barrel and every pair of hands available. The 1907 memory of that process is especially vivid. Mary was six. Sara was two-and-a-half. Witnessing the deep love which these 95 and 92-year-old sisters have for one another now (in 1997), it's hard to conceive that Mary could have thrown a big cabbage head at little Sara! But her flamboyant anger had its moment! A huge pile of cabbage heads were cleaned and trimmed, waiting to be shredded. Mary's hands are painfully arthritic now, but that day they were strong, supple, and determined! Her aim was perfect. Had she not played baseball with her brothers many times? The cabbage flew across the room, hitting its target all too well. Sara's vocal chords bellowed, and her head started to swell. No doubt Mama tended to the wound first, but Mary can only remember the sound of her feet, running out to get a strong switch from a peach tree branch. Mary's wails joined Sara's in a cacophonous, doleful chorus. Fortunately, the switch must have been a Proverbial one which would have won King Solomon's approval. Mary did not die, but she never needed a peach tree-branch-switching again. The last one left too good an impression. Sitting down was less comfortable for a while!

Anger is often accompanied by tears, but usually shed by the angry one. Almost anything could make young Mary's temper flare. One day she found her beloved Mama crying as if her heart would break. "Why are you crying, Mama?" she asked with sympathetic appeal. "Because you get so angry, Mary dear! I don't know what will become of you!" Those tears are precious to Mary even to this day. However, her brothers and sisters had an explanation, plausible to them, for Mary's weakness. "Mary gets angry," they claimed, "because John Hager brought her to us on his balky horse!" Mr. Hager is not alive to protest the connection, so some little explanation must suffice. Mr. Hager was an itinerant preacher, visiting the Haas home the night that Mary was born, the sixth of the eight arrows in Jacob's quiver. Mr. Hager had arrived on a white horse which the kids nicknamed, "Balky," as he was rather obstreperous, to say the very least.

Mary's siblings' excuse for her weakness, however, failed to out-live the experience Mary had in 1913 when she was twelve years old. She attended a revival meeting at a country church, one mile from the Haas home. The Gospel of Christ's death, burial, and resurrection on behalf of sinners was elucidated faithfully. The preacher winsomely gave an invitation at the end of the service, asking any one needing Christ to come forward in response to His love. Mary must have tangibly laid her propensity for anger at the altar when she invited Christ to be her personal Savior and Lord. Her Sunday School teacher prayed with her as she wholeheartedly accepted the gift of new life in Christ.

> *"If any one is in Christ, he (or she) is a new creation; the old has gone, the new has come! All this is from God" –*
> *2 Cor. 5:17.*

With that monumental decision to turn the reins of her life over to Christ, the last vestige of angry, balky episodes vanished. To God belongs the glory!

* * * * * * *

> *"Live by the Spirit, and you will not gratify the desires of the sinful nature...The acts of the sinful nature are obvious...fits of rage... dissensions...But the fruit of the Spirit is love, joy, peace, patience, kindness, goodness, faithfulness, gentleness and self-control" – Gal. 5:19-22.*

The Haas family homestead.

Baby Milford Haas, 18 months old, enjoying Mary's sisterly touch. She is 15 months older.

Mary and Sara Haas, about 10 and 8 years old.

2

"Daddy's Little Missionary"

Who can measure the value of the legacy of a happy childhood? The special preciousness of "belonging," of being deeply loved, of being taught time-tested moral values, of having one's actual needs supplied (but not necessarily all the "wants"), of having the long-term companionship of brothers and sisters, of taking part from an early age in assuming family responsibilities, and of learning accountability in a closely-knit arena of mutual understanding? The answer is unequivocally, "No one!" Those assets, whose value is appreciated far more at age 95 than they could have been at age 5 or 15, are Mary Haas' legacy from a godly parentage. Learning to love God supremely, developing an insatiable delight in the inexhaustible treasures of the Word of God, daily witnessing the efficacy of family prayers, and the intangible, but eternal dividends of godly living — those are Mary's riches for time and eternity.

From a very early age, Mary housed within her heart the desire to be a missionary. Her father, being a lay pastor, preached missions, and her mother, always hospitable, invited many missionaries passing through Pandora to share their humble home and their meals. So Mary had an early exposure to what missionaries and their ministry were like.

Quite a contrast to my own personal experience! I had never met a missionary, nor read a missions book until well after I had accepted the Lord at the age of 17. My very first personal confrontation with the scary concept of missions came in the form of a proposal of marriage from a Bible School student who had just surrendered his life to God for service in Africa. The incident occurred quite a while before I had considered entering Bible School and preparing for service. My entire view of missions and Africa was, sad to say, narrowly prejudiced by the Tarzan films I had seen in the movie theatres. I did not accept the proposal. Thankfully, my viewpoint about Missions and Africa was to change completely later on. Enough digression!

Back: Walter, Harvey, Mary, Albert, Milford
Front: Sara, Mama, Daddy, Clara
Photo taken when Mary was leaving to enter Moody Bible Institute in 1922.

Let's get acquainted with the beloved people with whom Mary's life was shaped. We've already met Jacob, her father, who was born in 1867. He was an enterprising farmer and lay-preacher who held his title as head of the home very graciously, winning respect, love and obedience. As pastor to the family as well as to his congregation, he fed them faithfully the eternal words of life, and introduced them to Jesus, the Bread of Life and the Water of Life. Jacob's mother's name, Mary, was given to his sixth child who became, like the Lord's mother, the "hand-maid of the Lord." Mary Minnie Haas reiterated the words of her who was "blessed among women" many times when seeking God's solution to a problem, as she said, "Be it unto me according to your will."

Mary's middle name, Minnie, was given in honor of her mother's sister, Minnie. Sarah Augsburger Haas, her mother, was a gentle woman, well-mannered, undemonstrative, but a hard worker, and a faithful molder of character. She was born in 1872. She bore eight children, never complaining about the increase in the work-load, but rather training the older children to help in the care of the younger ones. She fed all of them well. Only one of the eight failed to reach adulthood. That was Homer, the third child, who succumbed at age 17 to an enlargement of his spleen. Homer was a dedicated Christian. Sarah cared for him lovingly throughout his long illness. On the last day of his life, he asked her, "Can't you hear the beautiful singing of the angels?" When she admitted that she could not, he became just a bit impatient with her. The singing was overwhelmingly beautiful in his ears, and he was sure it must be audible to her as well. It was then that she realized that he would not live to see another day dawn, and she was right. Mary was only 10 years old when dear Homer left a vacancy in the family circle. He was greatly missed.

Walter was the first child born to Jacob and Sarah. He became a farmer. Mary enjoyed watching the progression of his romance with Ella Spallinger. The couple were married by Jacob in Ella's home, as all of the Haas family excitedly participated in the first of the many family marriages which were to follow. Walter and Ella had three children. How thrilled Mary was when her first niece was born—LaDonna, who would become Mrs. Bob Matthewson. Walter lived only one-half mile from the country schoolhouse which Mary and her siblings attended, so every chance they got, they dashed over to vie with one another to hold baby LaDonna. She was a beauty! With so many aunts and uncles to dote over her, it's a wonder that she wasn't spoiled. She is one of the very few relatives of Mary whom I have met, and Mary has shared her delightful niece and nephew with me quite a few times. She and her husband live only 50 miles from us.

Mary's first two nieces, LaDonna and Lenna on either side of Mary.
Left: LaDonna's husband, Bob, and Lenna's daughter, Sue.

LaDonna's younger sister, Lenna, whom, happily, I have also met, was born after Walter and family had moved away from Pandora. Mary didn't have the chance to spend time with Lenna as she had had with LaDonna. But when Walter's son, Virgil, was born, Mary and Ella's sister went to his home to help in the care of Ella and Virgil. There she saw more of Lenna and LaDonna. That experience was fun! For more reasons than one. Two neighbor boys noticed the two nursemaids in the Haas home, and asked them for dates! So changing diapers didn't occupy all of their time! Virgil became a big-time dairyman with extensive land and cattle. He died at a comparatively young age.

Mary's oldest sister, Clara, followed Walter into the Jacob and Sarah Haas family. Her husband was Enos Walter. Clara was a good big sister to Mary, even into adulthood. She had one son, Kenneth, whose wife was Vera, who gave Clara her only grandchild, Wilma, who is still living at this writing.

Harvey was the fourth Haas child. He became a carpenter and lumber entrepreneur. He married Edna Price, and had a son, Bob. Bob's wife, Peggy, has remained a very loyal member of the Haas family, even though Bob was called to Glory some years ago. She keeps in close touch with Mary, Milford, and Sara, the only three living children of the Jacob Haas family. She has been a loving mother to her daughter, Debbie. I enjoyed visiting Peggy in her lovely home in 1993 when Mary, Helen Vetter and I went to Pandora to visit Milford.

What a variety of professions emerged from that Jacob Haas family! Albert, the fifth child, became an excellent mechanic. He and his wife are no longer living, nor is their son, Duane. But a daughter, Marjorie Fruchey, is alive and has two daughters, Sue Hall and Linda Lochart—both great-neices to Mary.

Mary, number 6, was followed 15 months later by Milford. Milford had an illustrious career as a businessman, even being elected the most successful businessman in Pandora one year. He owned a funeral service and a furniture store, but kept his spiritual duties in excellent perspective, serving in the St. John Mennonite Church as a deacon, elder, and missions committeeman. He was well-loved by the Pandora people. His first wife, Inez Lehman, died of heart trouble. They adopted an only son, Marvin, born in 1943, whom they loved dearly. Milford went through very deep sorrow when the Police reported to him that Marvin had been killed in an auto accident in 1971, seven weeks after Inez's death! He later married Inez's brother's wife, Vera. After Vera's

Mary, Milford, Sara and Harvey (deceased). Taken about 1990.

death, Mary spent six months with him, helping him to make the adjustment to living alone. He managed for some years until age left its mark upon him. He rather hesitantly agreed to the inevitable. and entered the Bluffton Mennonite Nursing Home in 1995 where he remains. He is getting excellent care now (1997) at age 93. Peggy and Lenna visit him regularly. Mary calls the nurses every week to get an update on his well-being, and every year, as strength allows, she goes out to visit him. He has been a tower of strength and encouragement to her all through the years, helping her in many practical ways, including supplying her with several cars. There's a beautiful bond between the three remaining Haases—Mary, Milford, and Sara.

Sara was the eighth Haas baby, born 15 months after Milford. Sara became Mrs. Ernest Francis. She had no children, but she was an ideal partner for Ernest. They lived in Detroit, Michigan, and then in Long Beach, California where Ernest died of a heart attack. Sara supported herself by working as a dress saleslady in a large department store where she soon became very popular with her clients. Her personality is very outgoing, so folks are easily drawn to her. Her love of fun and constant activity is contagious. She is known all over her area for her expertise in bowling. She has won so many silver cups that she feels constrained to put them out on the curb for whoever wants them, since her small apartment can't house them indefinitely. If her score doesn't reach 200 consistently, she moans that she's too old to bowl anymore! When she appears at a bowling alley, the teams vie with one another to have her on their side. One day she was driving past a bowling alley and spied a big banner with bold letters, declaring, "Sara Francis bowls here!" So far, much to my regret, I've missed the blessing of meeting her, except by phone.

About a year ago Sara arrived home after having helped some friend with an estate clearing. (She has helped many friends with such tasks, and has chauffeured many to doctor appointments, etc). To her dismay, she realized that she had forgotten to take along her apartment keys. She circled the building, looked up to the second floor where her apartment was located and saw that a window was left open a bit. She is the Custodian for the building which houses six apartments, so she knew where to go to get a ladder. She summoned some one to come to steady the ladder while she climbed up to the window on the second floor, pushed open the window further, and squeezed her 92-year-old-body through safely. In a few moments, she was down again to put the ladder away. Mary begs her to give up her job as custodian, but her appeals reach unwilling ears. She continues carrying out huge garbage cans, sweeping the premises, collecting the rents, and even nursing the sick tenants or feeding them when they need help. That Haas stock is feisty! So feisty that Sara packs and delivers "Meals on Wheels" four times weekly! A picture she sent to Mary shows ultra-thin Sara trying to give her burly "Meals on Wheels" driver a hug. Several yards of extensions on her arms would be needed to encircle that jovial driver! Every guest to Mary's apartment must see that picture which never fails to bring a hearty laugh. And Mary does love to laugh!

Jacob Haas had a brother, John. His three children, Grace, Katherine, and Milton, were close cousins to Mary. They lived in the Fort Myers area, and visited back and forth quite often with Mary in Sebring, Florida. In 1996 Milton passed away, and Grace and Katherine followed him to Glory in 1997.

Viola Welty is another cousin. She is the only relative who was also a member of the SIM. She served in Nigeria for about nine years, and then married Herbert Peters. Several years after Mary's mother died in 1943, Jacob married Viola's mother, and thus Viola became a step-sister as well as a cousin!

As stated, Mary's brother, Homer, died as a young man. All the other family members—grandparents, parents, siblings, and in-laws, died while Mary was in Africa, unable to attend the funerals, with the exception of Harvey's. He died several years ago, but Mary was ill and unable to go to Ohio from Florida. Harvey left his widow, Lottie, who is still living at this writing. Knowing a bit about Mary's background makes her friends appreciate her that much more!

On the SIM Retirement Village compound Mary is not only the oldest resident, but probably the most beloved. She is a living magnet, drawing folks to drop in for a visit. Most of them see pictures of her family and of her "Queen for a Day" experience on TV, and oh, yes, they don't get over the doorsill again without signing her guest book, which is the fourth one she has had since living in Sebring. It's a good record of visitors' travels, addresses, and phone numbers. Sometimes she finds a little remark about an excellent meal or a funtime, playing games, and Mary delights in such memorabilia. Dozens of cars with Ohio licenses on them have parked outside her door. She doesn't drive herself anymore, but travels with me very often, and I tease her about always being able to spot an Ohio license in traffic, but never able to find a New Jersey one to remind me of my roots.

Cousins gather to celebrate Mary's 80th birthday.
Left to right: Grace and Katherine Haas, Vera and Evelyn Steiner, Mary's sister, Sara,
freind, Ruth Veenker, and the new octogenarian. (12/31/81)

3

Decision Clinched

Daddy's little missionary watched as her older siblings enjoyed the romantic fantasies and realities of their teens and twenties. Soon it was Mary's turn to be the object of the approving glances, the invitations to dates, the flutters, the teasing, the assessing of the various companions, and the enjoyment of the attention directed her way. Subtly, normal womanly desire to be prince charming's "one and only" and a homemaker started to surface, squelching those taken-for-granted missionary aspirations. It wasn't a teenage rebellion at all. It wasn't a matter of a wild spree, involving devious behavior. The dates were innocent enough: mainly invitations to church, young people's activities, skating, movies, and such like. But the heart's priorities were shifting gradually away from the image of herself as a pioneer missionary on some neglected continent. Visions of bridal veil and gown, "I Do's" and scattered confetti showed up in her waking dreams in ever-increasing measure. Rather normal. Nothing to be ashamed of. Part of growing up.

Then, suddenly at age 17 or 18 the dreams were nestled in pillows, wet with feverish perspiration. Phlebitis in her knee spread throughout her body, and immobilized her for seven weeks. The family doctor summoned a specialist who pronounced her case the worst he had seen. It was serious. One day the family doctor called her mother outside and sadly related his worst fears. He doubted that Mary could live through the day. Her mother did not want to hide the truth from Mary, so she went back to her bed and tearfully told her the doctor's prediction. But then Mama called Daddy, who was ploughing corn. He tied the horses to a fence and dashed to Mary's bedside. All of the family was summoned. Every one stood around Mary's bed. In turn, each one prayed. Daddy committed Mary to God's loving care, and promised that if it pleased the Lord to spare her to regain her health, he and Mama would do everything in their power to help her to get wherever He wanted her to serve Him. Harvey was the only immediate family member not present. He was in the Service. World

War I was being waged. He got permission to go home immediately.

Mary was too ill to pray aloud, but in her heart she formulated her resolve to forfeit her preoccupation with being married. She would go wherever the Lord wanted her to be, should He see fit to restore her to health.

At noon the doctor called to check on Mary's condition. Mama said she detected a change for the better. He returned at 2:00 p.m. and triumphantly declared, "She will make it! She'll live!" As steady improvement was seen day by day he said, "Mary is my miracle patient!"

About six months later, Mary felt like herself again. She applied for a job as telephone operator in Pandora, was accepted, and started her on-the job training. To implement her decision to serve the Lord, she enrolled in a Moody Bible Institute Correspondence Course from Chicago. It was that famous, formidable, time-consuming course called "Synthesis," which every Moody alumnus remembers well. Quite a challenge! It whetted her appetite for full-time Bible study, so in the Fall of 1922 she enrolled as a day student at Moody, "The West Point of Christian Service." New students were required to report with enough money to pay for the first semester's room, board and books. The Pandora job had made that possible. Every Moody student since 1886 until the present has thanked God for the faithful donors who have supported the school's policy of offering tuition-free education in preparation for Christian service. Room, board, and textbook expenses, however, loomed large on students' minds at the end of the first semester. Mary was no exception. She went to the assigned advisor and said she would like assistance in obtaining part-time employment. "What experience have you had, Miss Haas?" was the advisor's query. "I am a telephone operator," was her quick reply. "Splendid!" Click, click click and the right person was contacted to enroll Mary to work at the main desk of the "153 Building," (Original building which

Jacob and Sarah Haas with Mary upon her departure for Moody Bible Institute, Chicago, 1922.

was the address of the Institute for many years). Mary was to work on Sunday afternoons and evenings, and also to work a full day every Monday. Her wages? Fourty-eight dollars a month, just enough to cover her board! Oh, for such figures today!

Moody Bible Institute has been since its inception, and continues to be, unique in providing a Practical Work Program which gives students invaluable experience in various types of ministry. I can't speak for today, but in past years it was required that every student participate twice a week in specified assignments. Those experiences, some with one partner, and some as a team, overcame natural reticence and bashfulness and feelings of insecurity. Chicago is a large city which has felt the immense impact of students' ministry in the jails, hospitals, nursing homes, homes for unwed mothers, in churches, Sunday Schools, rescue missions, Child Evangelism classes, and in door-to-door visitation. Mary profited greatly from her exposure to these city ministries, so different from her rural background experience. As every missionary knows, the Lord uses every exposure to experience in life in some distinct way on the mission field. Moody's Practical Work Department, now bearing a different name, was often remembered with gratitude.

The Missionary Union was another wonderful part of student life. Every Saturday night the entire student body met for a missions-emphasis rally, with special music and a challenge from some part of God's Harvest Field. Before a student graduated, he had been exposed to real-life missionaries from every part of the globe, had seen pictures, and had been able to assess his own potential place for service. In addition to the Saturday meeting, there were ten "Prayer Bands," led by students interested in a particular part of the world. Up-to-date prayer requests, geographical and social situations were reported upon covering China, Japan, the Islands of the world, Africa, America, Latin America, Europe, Asia, Jewish work, and Australia/New Zealand. These meetings were elective, in contrast to the Saturday night rally when attendance was a part of the curriculum. Each prayer band met once a week, some right after breakfast and some after lunch from Monday through Friday. They were a means of unlimited broadening of information about the needs of the world. Learning to intercede on behalf of people very different from those already known was a new experience for most students—an enriching one.

Mary attended the prayer bands and was especially drawn to the need of Russia, probably in large part because one of the students with whom she had become friendly had come to Moody from Russia. So Mary started to "zero in" on Russia as her probable future home.

In the course of time Dr. Hughes, the Secretary of SIM, came to Moody. He issued a rousing challenge, stating SIM's need for 100 new missionaries that year. Mary dutifully added that urgent request to her prayer list, but did not consider that the challenge affected her. During her devotions one day as she brought the need to the Lord, she knew that He was saying to her, "Why not you?" "Oh no, Lord," she answered quickly, "I'm going to Russia!" Easy words to articulate, but the after-effect of having blithely said, "Oh no, Lord," robbed her of her peace of mind. She hadn't actually articulated the real reason for not wanting to go to Africa, as it sounded just a bit trite, and it wouldn't be information that the Lord didn't already know. When the lack of peace became acute, she returned to her trysting-place with the Lord and said, "Yes, I'll go to Africa if that's where you want me—smells or no smells!" Her restless spirit was soothed by her own submission, and peace returned.

Mary became acquainted with other future SIMers, Mrs. Harry Harling, the first Mrs. David Osborne, and Mrs. Leslie Tuller. All of them were single ladies at the time, and headed for service in Africa under SIM. Their fellowship was very helpful to Mary in her new decision. The men to whom the three ladies were engaged were already in Africa, awaiting their arrivals.

Before graduating in April of 1925, Mary applied to the Sudan Interior Mission. She was invited to go to Collingswood, Ontario, Canada as a candidate in September of that same year. She was to meet the Council and have some orientation, getting acquainted with the Mission in-depth. All of the candidates had to have a thorough physical exam to assess the prospect that their health would be amenable to living in the tropics. The doctor reported to the Council that Miss Haas' lungs were not strong enough to endure life in Africa; perhaps China, but not Africa. Mary wasn't told about that opinion.

The Council members, the SIM staff, and all the candidates went to a park shortly after the physical exams for a picnic and ball game. Remember, please, that Mary grew up with five brothers! She was a seasoned baseball player. She entered this game as her usual self, full of pep, vim, and vigor, and unaware that she was being watched. She yelled so loudly and played so heartily that the watching Council members said, "There's nothing wrong with Mary's lungs! She can go to Africa!" Mary often claims that her 43 years of service in Africa stemmed from a baseball game.

While at Moody, Mary had not taken the Missionary-Medical course, but had had a first-aid course. That was hardly sufficient to prepare her to grapple with the difficult medical needs in a tropical country. Like many others, she wanted to go on to full nurses' training for better preparation for the tough cases out there, often handled by those with very little training. But Dr. Rowland Bingham, the Founder and Director of the Sudan Interior Mission said to her, "We need missionaries right now!" So Mary returned from Canada, formally accepted as an appointee, to make preparations for an early December sailing.

Mary's father had been the Lay Pastor of the Swiss Mennonite Church in Pandora, Ohio. During Mary's student days at Moody, that home church disbanded in favor of attending a church where English was the dominant teaching language. Mary's entire family joined the St. John Mennonite Church in Pandora, and Mary's membership was transferred in absentia. The ladies of that church rejoiced in the calling of their new member to missionary service, and made all of Mary's clothes for her projected four-year term of ministry. They sewed a beautiful quilt for her, as only Mennonite ladies can do, and provided other necessities. The church did not assume the financial support of Mary at that time. But during her second furlough, around 1935, they took up responsibility for a large part of the support, and continue to do so even to the present. Mary's gratitude knows no bounds for those close bonds with neighbors and friends whom she can rely on for prayer backing as well as for some of the necessary monthly support money sent to the mission.

Mary gathered up all the other items mentioned on the "Outfit List," and she proceeded to New York City in November of 1925.

Up to that time, the SIM Headquarters had been solely in Canada, but Mary's arrival in New York coincided with the acquisition of a Brooklyn, New York Headquarters on Garfield Place. She was part of the very first party to leave for Africa from Brooklyn. While waiting to leave, the eight girls in the group, including the three Moody friends mentioned above, placed all the furniture in the rooms of the new headquarters. A new experience! She is the only survivor of that party of eight.

The night before they were to sail, a Brooklyn church held a farewell service for them, with Dr. Rowland Bingham, SIM's General Director, speaking. Each of the eight girls gave her testimony. An offering was received. The remaining sum of money needed for the travel expenses was fully met. What a lovely seal on God's call and timing!

The eight sailed the next day on an American ship. The December winds didn't allow them adequate time to stand on the deck, watching the awesome power of God, controlling the heaving waves. They reached England after eight days, and stayed there two weeks, shopping for tropical supplies which were not easily found in the U.S. at that time. To add to their list of "firsts", they were the first SIM party to arrive at the new Liverpool Home. Mr. Jack Nicholson from New Zealand, Mr. Bill Collins from Canada, and a Mr. Nelson joined their group, as well as two British ladies. They sailed on an Elder-Dempster ship headed for Lagos where they arrived on December 10th, 1925. Mary celebrated her 24th birthday at the upcountry Minna Language School on December 31, 1925. That school was where new recruits studied the Hausa language. Hausa has been of tremendous blessing as a "lingua franca" throughout a very large part of West Africa. It crosses many tribal barriers and is used as a mother-tongue for the Hausa tribe as well as a market language for many other tribes.

Mary soon learned that she was being assigned to work with the Jaba tribe, so there was no need for her to remain at Minna. She traveled by train to a railroad junction at Jagindi. Mr. Tom Allen came to meet her from Kurmin Musa, a station only 15 miles distant from her assigned station, K'woi. There her first real taste of African life began—one entirely outmoded now. She was carried in a hammock by porters who had accompanied Mr. Allen from Kurmin Musa. Mr. Allen rode his bicycle as Mary was trying to endure the constant swaying back and forth, totally unable to understand the jabber of the carriers. They went on "bush" paths through jungle. Sometimes she gasped as she thought her head might be caught in overhanging branches of trees or bushes. She hoped that no one would step on a snake and drop her hammock in running from it. Plenty of bugs kept her company. Her tummy felt like it was still on the high seas at times. But finally, the carriers were greeted by voices of their friends at Kurmin Musa, and they babbled and laughed, louder and faster. Mary was more than relieved when they put her carry-cot down on terra firma.

Getting her upright equilibrium after a long ride of perpetual motion wasn't easy, but she had to snap to alertness to answer the kindly greetings of Mrs. Tom Allen and Miss Annie Wighton, Scottish veterans at Kurmin Musa. She learned that she would be staying at Kurmin Musa for a period of time, due to the fact that the only missionary at K'woi was Mr. Tom Watson, a bachelor waiting for his wedding date.

Mary's time at Kurmin Musa proved to be providential, as she learned a very great deal from the Allens and Miss Wighton. The day after her arrival, Mrs. Allen put Mary to work at the Dispensary. She was a fine nurse, highly-experienced, and with a distinct gift for teaching plebs what she knew. Mary credits that personal induction into the world of missionary medicine for her having obtained the government certificate of qualification to run a dispensary. The Allens and Miss Wighton gave her a valued foundation for her ministry at K'woi. When furlough time came around for the Allens, it was deemed best that Mary stay with Miss Wighton at Kurmin Musa, as the Mission did not like to leave a single lady alone on a station. Mary tried to keep up with the heavy work schedule of the hyperactive Miss Wighton, but by the end of 3 3/4 years of her first four-year term, weakness developed and the doctor sent her home a bit early to recuperate.

Upon arrival in New York, Mary boarded a train for Ohio and was met by her parents and the rest of the family. The winter weather in Ohio was not conducive to a quick recovery, so the family decided to go to Florida for the rest of the winter. They went to Fort Myers where one of Mary's uncles lived. Mary became acquainted with many new friends, including the Bealls who assumed part of her support and have generously continued with it even to this day. What a record of faithfulness as stewards—68 years! Mary had time to anticipate her work at K'woi, and she was anxious to return to Africa.

Previously, Mary had not had supporters. When it came time for her to return to Africa, funds for her trip were not on hand. By the Lord's gracious provision, Annie Wighton, who was on furlough in Scotland, reported Mary's need to her dear friends, Mr. and Mrs. Ewing. Immediately Mr. Ewing, who already had extensive monetary commitments on behalf of other missionaries, including Annie, jumped at the opportunity to assist this American woman whom Annie had described in glowing terms. He said to Annie, "I have only one requisite. Miss Haas must come to our home in Scotland to visit us during her return trip to Africa." A letter, written with alacrity by the excited Annie, crossed the Atlantic to the small town of Pandora, Ohio. It heralded the happy news to Mary about the prospect of further reliable financial and spiritual help for her next term of service. At the end of her furlough Mary embarked for Scotland and was met by her gracious Scottish hosts who escorted her to their imposing home. She spent two memorable weeks listening to their delightful Scottish brogue, and relating to them her family background and the experiences of her first term of service in Nigeria. A very deep bond developed between them. The Ewings provided what was lacking in her passage account, and sent to the SIM a small portion of Mary's support needs. They continued to do so until they were called Home to Heaven.

After two weeks in Scotland, Mary went on her way to the adventures of her assignment to K'woi station in northern Nigeria, thankful for new prayer helpers. That big decision which she had clinched at age 17 or 18 was to bear abundant fruit for God's glory.

Mr. and Mrs. Ewing of Scotland

4

Daughter of the Tribe

Mary's original assignment had been to a Jaba tribe town called K'woi. But her first term of service was spent at Kurmin Musa where the Jaba language was also spoken. Her biggest task during that time was in learning the language, which she did creditably. After the memorable first furlough, she was as eager as a race horse to reach the place of her own assignment, about 15 miles from Kurmin Musa. She had learned a great deal while there, and was chomping at the bit to gallop into new experiences at this "bush" (rural) station in the north-central part of Nigeria. At that time Nigeria was a British Colony, not divided into separate regions or states, but simply into "north" and "south."

The resident missionaries at K'woi, Mr. and Mrs. William Watson, were hardy Scottish workers. They both welcomed Mary warmly, happy to have a co-worker with whom to share the burgeoning work of the station. The K'woi people are drawn to new arrivals like bees to honey. They swarmed around to assure her of their welcome. After a good inspection of this slim lady with the big smile, they named her *Tiri K'woi,* the daughter of K'woi, a great honor not bestowed lightly. Africans have amazing discernment of character. Once in a while, an affixed name can reflect a negative impression such as one vernacular name which alerted people to the fact that the person so-named was given to anger. Fortunately, the real intent of the name was never understood by the one accused of anger, but the tribes people knew. Mr. Thomas Archibald, who had labored at K'woi for a short time, had been named *Dacip*, which means in Jaba "the merry one," as he was a fun-lover. His wife was called *Dariya*, "laughter".

Mary was the first American missionary to arrive at K'woi. There was, from the start, a very cordial relationship between her and her seniors, but when the Watsons' little son, Bertie (pronounced "bear-tee") started chattering, using American expressions, the Scottish parents became a wee bit perturbed. Mary was soon quite conscious of the wide Atlantic's divisive influence. The speech of Americans takes a lot of getting used to by Britishers, so she tried to exercise control of colloquialisms learned from her youth. Another adjustment: an entirely different way of handling table cutlery! In order not to confuse the alert, impressionable little Bertie, Mary started eating like a true Britisher, and actually got convinced that their system was more sensible than ours! She still reverts to it more often than not. The next worker to arrive at K'woi was Daisy Law, a "bonnie Scottish lassie," so she didn't have to make the cultural adjustments which Mary had faced so far as inter-staff matters were concerned. Daisy was not there very long, as she married a man from another mission and moved away.

K'woi was to be Mary's home for 23 years. For the last ten of those years she had the responsibility of being the station head, since the Watsons had returned to Scotland permanently. Her four co-workers were Eva Doerksen from California, Elsie Hendricksen from Alberta, Canada, Yuni Coquerel from England, and Ruth Veenker from Iowa. They were a wonderful team, each one's ministry complementing that of the others.

The K'woi S.I.M. church had the largest number of Christians in Northern Nigeria at that time — about 175 Believers. It became a pattern church, and a wonderful source of personnel for new stations and churches emerging in various places. It also supplied missionaries of other stations with domestic helpers, as every one was glad to employ a Christian, if possible. So the K'woi witness spread in unplanned ways.

Mary's home was a small round mud-brick hut with a thatched roof (grass), while the Watsons lived in the "main house," a mud-brick rectangular building. One day, during a heavy rainstorm, Mary saw, through her tiny hut window, lightning strike the Watson house, with the Watsons inside. The roof burst into flames. Nationals were quick to detect the danger, and rushed in to assist. They climbed up to pull down the smoldering bamboo poles which supported the grass roof. The ceiling was made of split palm logs, covered with mud which, fortunately, helped to contain the fire. Often fine lines divide tragedy from humor, and such was the case that day. As the nationals were struggling with the roof, groaning, huffing and puffing, they spied a rabbit running across the compound. Every one of the men postponed his fire-extinguishing, jumped down from the roof, and ran after the hapless rabbit who didn't stand a chance of survival. They finished their job, and their reward was a tasty portion of rabbit meat. Any kind of meat would have been a treat, but rabbit tasted like chicken, and they savored every bite, licking their chops and enjoying the memory of fire fighting, combined with rabbit-chasing.

Mary's first job at K'woi was teaching any and all who wanted to learn to read, from toddlers to totterers. One old grandfather was learning to count. He used his fingers to get to ten, and then unceremoniously lifted up his skinny legs and started counting his crusty toes which had never nestled into a pair of shoes. Gleefully, he got to twenty, but then ran out of digits!

Later Mary took on the medical work, caring for a large clientele of local patients. Bruises, cuts, ulcers, rotting teeth, tummy aches, rashes, snake bites, and childbirths challenged her short medical missionary training obtained at Moody Bible Institute. She also treated many leprosy patients.

In addition, lacking a man to plan and supervise the multiple building projects, Mary drew on instinct, observation, wise advice, and good sense rather than on specific training in order to oversee the erection and upkeep of forty buildings in the K'woi area. However, her devotion to the routine grind of responsibilities did not stifle her evangelistic zeal. Fortunately, she had learned to ride a horse as a teenager, so she rode horseback to neighboring villages as time allowed.

Some time later, Mary imported a gasoline-powered, three-wheeled scooter. Nigerian Customs officials were thrown into a quandry. Since it was the first vehicle of its kind to roll its wheels on Nigerian soil, under what category should they register it? They examined it with intense curiosity before deciding that it was somewhat like a motorcycle, so it was written under that dubious classification. Their hesitancy was no doubt a factor in the waiving of fees!

On an early scooter trip to Jos, where the Nigeria Headquarters of SIM were located, Mary jostled over 30 miles of the bumpy bush paths, being covered with dust before arriving at Kafanchan. There she and her scooter boarded a train, bound for Jos, about 70 miles away. Upon arrival, she was an *abin kallo* (something to stare at) as she rode the scooter to the SIM compound. The next morning she climbed into her trusty three-wheeler again, heading for the famous Jos Market where anything and everything could be found in wild profusion. Alas, her approach on the chugging scooter aroused folks all along the road. A huge crowd soon surrounded her, jabbering in various vernaculars. No chance to pass them! To her relief, two men in police uniforms emerged from the crowd of onlookers. They took upon themselves the task of clearing a path for Mary and her scooter. The crowd was left behind to wonder if a Martian had descended, or what. They had never before seen a scooter, much less a woman driver!

One day Mary heard her cook's hearty laugh. He was just coming to work, and blurted out, "I heard a remark in the town which will make you laugh!" "What did you hear?" Mary asked, her curiosity well aroused. "That scooter of yours is the offspring of your big truck! The truck gave birth, and the scooter is the progeny!" Mary, always ready for a good laugh, willingly obliged.

Mary's co-workers, Eva, Elsie, Yuni, and Ruth contributed greatly to the overall impact of the work at K'woi. Eva conducted Bible classes which eventually developed into a large Bible School which is still functioning at K'woi. It has trained scores of evangelists and pastors to teach the Word of God, first in the Hausa language and later in English. Elsie was a "trekker," spending most of her time in village evangelism and nurturing of Christians in the Word at their local settings. Yuni cared for a contingency of orphans. Ruth Veenker started an Elementary School, and later a Senior Primary School. A Secondary School (High School) came later, and a Girls' Senior Primary.

Byang Kato was just a little boy when Mary was at K'woi. He loved to have the privilege of carrying Mary's phonograph wherever she went to preach or teach children. Little could she have envisioned how he would emerge to become a well-known speaker on several continents. He came to the U.S.A. to study at Dallas Theological Seminary where he attained a Ph.D. with his thesis on the danger of syncretism in the church, being taught on so many fronts. That philosophy encouraged the extraction of the best from every religion, and the mixture of all together. It aimed at establishing a religion on a third-world continent which would supposedly be relevant and acceptable to all. It cared nothing about the forfeiture of the indispensable, eternally-relevant truths of God's written revelation found in the Holy Bible. Byang Kato fought for the dynamism of unfettered Truth to remain available in every language on every continent for all people. He became the Executive Secretary of a very important inter-church organization, head-quartered in Kenya and serving all of Africa. It was while he was in Kenya in that post that he drowned in the ocean. He was mourned by all who knew him. The author of this book knew him well as a young man who loved to write letters to the editor of **Labarin Ekklesiya** or **Kakaki**, the Hausa magazines serving the churches throughout Hausa-speaking Nigeria and Niger. He wrote many, and I answered every one, so appreciative of his keen interest. Byang Kato's life-story is in book form, available through the offices of the SIM. It was written by the late Sophie de la Haye. "The memory of the just is blessed."

Hadassa memorized the Gospel of Mark as Mary read it to her.

As stated, Mary Haas delighted to teach reading to any one eager to learn. Old Hadassa wanted to learn urgently. Mary read and reread to her the Gospel of Mark. She perfectly memorized the entire Gospel, but could not learn to read. But she "read" to others by memory the priceless treasures of Mark's account of the life and ministry of "the Son of Man who came to minister and to give His life a ransom for many" —Mark 10:45.

An unexpected ministry opened up for Mary when Mrs. Smith of the Church Missionary Society of England taught her to read Braille. Mary used that knowledge to teach a blind man, Batu, to read. He had gone blind when a curse was put on him by an angry person. Shortly after he became proficient in reading Braille, he arose in the worship service and read the scriptures to the church body on a Sunday morning. Every one was flabbergasted, including the pastor, as no one had ever heard or seen such a phenomenon. They wondered, did he go from being cursed to being endued with mysterious power in his fingers? No! But every new advance meets with incredulity, whether in our sophisticated society or in a less educated one. The blessing of Braille is immeasurable in Africa where blindness afflicts countless individuals.

Speaking of curses, Mary recalls an incident which occurred during her first term, spent at Kurmin Musa. Mrs. Allen was walking across a field of tall grass when she heard some moaning. She searched for the source of the sound, expecting to find an injured animal. Instead, it was a little boy, Hanaya, who had been bitten by a snake. His entire foot was swollen beyond recognition. It was one huge sore. She took him home and treated him. The animists there believed that any one who survived a snake-bite had an evil spirit and was under a curse. It took years of treatment by Mary and by others for Hanaya to be fully well, but he gave his heart to Christ and became an effectual evangelist. He was married, and matured as a powerful witness to the grace of God and the effect of love in action.

Another little K'woi boy of 10 or 12 years of age accepted Christ as His Savior in a Sunday School class. His parents were enraged. They forbid him to go to the class. But he persisted. They threw him into the goat hut, closed up the entrance with heavy logs, and left him there without mercy or food. The smells of an animal enclosure are not pleasant, but he patiently endured his situation. His grandmother was passing the goat hut and heard a voice penetrating the constant bleatings of the goats. She approached the hut and recognized the voice of her young grandson. She could hardly believe her ears as she listened to his distinct and fervent pleadings to God in prayer for his family. "Oh, God, please save my father!" "My mother doesn't know you love her. Have mercy on her!" "My grandmother is getting old and will die without forgiveness of her sins unless you save her." "The other children in the family haven't heard the wonderful stories I have heard about Jesus. Please let them go with me to Sunday School!" The grandmother was so deeply moved by his sincerity that she took the risk of arousing her son's wrath. She released the boy and took him to her small hut and shared her food with him. The father eventually agreed to her oversight of him. The grandmother gave her heart to the Lord, and soon became a member of Mary's Bible class for the elderly. She accompanied the church women on visits to homes and villages for preaching to those who had not heard the Gospel. How truly the Word declares that "A little child shall lead them."

Another little boy at K'woi accepted Christ and started attending the services regularly. Each time he returned home after a service he faced a hard whipping from his father, and was denied food for the rest of the day. After some time of repeated whippings and denial of food, the women of the church felt constrained to intervene. They decided to feed him before he left for home. In fact, they kept him at the church all day. Gradually the father acquiesced to the son's persistent faith, and assured him that he could return home without getting a beating. As far as Mary can recall, that little boy remained true to the Lord as the only Christian in his family.

* * * * * * *

"The disciples came to Jesus and asked, 'Who is the greatest in the kingdom of heaven?' He called a little child and had him stand among them. And he said, 'I tell you the truth, unless you change and become like little children, you will never enter the kingdom of heaven. Therefore, whoever humbles himself like this child is the greatest in the kingdom of heaven. And whoever welcomes a little child like this in my name welcomes me. But if any one causes one of these little ones who believe in me to sin, it would be better for him to have a large millstone hung around his neck and to be drowned in the depths of the sea'"— Matthew 18:1-6

One frame up! Mary supervised the building of the K'woi Church. The men on the roof are letting down a plumb line. They asked, "Why do you white people always want things straight? Did God ever make a straight tree?
Photo: L. Veenker

The first K'woi Elementary School, built under Mary's supervision. Ruth Veenker was the teacher.

Eva Doerksen and Mary, loyal coworkers for many years.

Mary, Elsie Hendricksen, and Ruth Veenker under the Jacaranda tree which was visible for four miles when in bloom.

Mary Haas with the first Christian woman at K'woi, also named Mary and Hadassa, helpers with the orphan babies.

5

Elephant-Ear Leaves! What For?

Much of Africa's activity, prosperity, industry, and perhaps even mental attitudes are seriously affected by the seasonal weather changes. The dry season can signal disaster for crops not yet matured, or those ripe for harvest, but lashed by an unseasonable rain or even hailstones. It can also usher in the long struggle with harmattan winds blowing southward from the Sahara Desert, covering everything with fine dust. The wet season can be the harbinger of mold on clothes and foods. Flu becomes rampant, and cold winds affect many people adversely, since they do not have heat in their homes, nor adequate clothing to withstand the sudden cold. Quite often fires are lit in their small mud-brick or thatch homes, and accidents occur, especially as small children may roll into the burning embers while sleeping. Conversely, however, the wet season also raises hopes for a good crop, so necessary for staving off hunger during the long dry season.

Almost without exception, every Jaba family in Nigeria was agrarian at the time that Mary lived at K'woi. Each family grew a large portion of their entire annual food supply during the wet season, and stored it in a granary for apportionment throughout the year.

When the rains started well, the eager farmers would rush to their farms in anticipation of enjoying the fruits of a very successful farming period. They hoped to reap a crop large enough to meet their own families' needs and perhaps even enough for a cash crop to sell at the local markets as well. The skies could change from cloudless clarity to black billows, driven by strong winds that could suddenly lift a person off his feet. The thunder clapped and rolled and shuddered, causing many moments of fear in little children's hearts. Unless one has heard torrential tropical rain teaming down upon a corrugated iron roof, wind banging windows and doors, branches and leaves of trees flying wildly, it may be difficult to conjure up a graphic image of this typical wet-season experience. It only rains here, but out in the tropics it pours! Lightning can be beautiful to behold, but often people are caught unprotected on open fields. Being struck by lightning is not as unusual there as it is in America.

Mary Haas, missionary to the Jaba people for 23 years, remembers vividly one particular rainy season. The early rains looked very promising. The crops were planted with enthusiastic optimism. Every ounce of the farmers' energy went into their plowing and sowing. They looked forward to a break from the hard manual work while the seeds took root and broke through the soil. Farmers there, as here, love the feel of the soil sifting through their fingers. The African farmers' toes and heels know that sensation, too! The rain in the air smells good. Moods are cheerful, and farmers are probably making early conjectures as to how much grain can be stored and how much sold. Alas! Weather can mock the wisest of plans! On this occasion the rains stopped abruptly. A severe dry spell ensued. The relentless heat of the tropical sun burnt everything to a crisp. The ground became as hard and inhospitable as it had been during the long dry season. What could be done? Wait and pray, and prepare to jump into action when the unpredictable season would possibly return to normal. With the next heavy rainfall they set to work again, repeating all the laborious steps to a good harvest. After some days, the buoyant hopes were dashed to dismal disappointment. They could only take comfort in the fact that they were not the only ones affected by the onset of another harsh dry spell.

The pagans (animists who believe in the concept of spirits residing in all natural phenomena and objects) gathered to invoke the spirits with loud wailing, drumming and horn blowing. The Muslims dutifully chanted over their prayer beads and repeated their creed, "There is no God but Allah, and Mohammed is the prophet of God." The Christians rallied together before daybreak in their mud-brick church to pray. Mary waited until daylight to join them there. As she approached the church, she was mystified to see what she had never seen before — a rather neat line-up of huge elephant-ear leaves, resting against the wall of the building. She entered the ante-room to pray with the elders. She asked, "Why are all those huge leaves lined up around the church? What use do they have?" The elders countered with their own question: "Didn't we come to pray for rain? Those leaves make wonderful umbrellas!" Though no rebuke had been intended, Mary did, indeed, feel the sting of remonstration. She set out to pray for rain, just as they had, but the thought of proving God by taking her umbrella had not occurred to her.

Mary and the elders entered the church and joined the congregation. They fell to their knees and engaged in fervent prayer that God would intervene on their behalf. They acknowledged His sovereignty over wind and weather, as well as over their souls. After about a half-hour of united prayer, a terrific clap of thunder shook the place, followed by a heavy downpour of rain — so loud that they could no longer hear one another's petitions. The head elder, Madaki, arose and thanked the Lord for His faithfulness in answering their prayer. He closed the meeting amid the sounds of praise.

The people retrieved their trusty leaves outside, held them over their heads, and joyously went to their homes, blessed by yet another assurance that their God loved them and cared about the details of their lives. They arrived home, not only happy in the Lord, but also dry! Mary was the only one who got soaked to her skin.

Mary, when you pray for rain again, please carry an umbrella! Or, at least, a huge leaf with a long stem!

6

To Chase, or to Pray ?

Madaki, Malam Maude, the first pastor of K'woi church.   Poto: L. Veenker.

All farmers everywhere dread the vagaries of weather and plagues which can wipe out many months' labors in a spellbindingly short period of time. All too well known among African farmers are the swarming locusts. As winged adults they are carried by the wind hundreds of miles from their breeding grounds. Upon landing, they devour **all** vegetation. Even small swarms can cover several square miles and weigh thousands of tons! They can consume their total weight in a day. Flying at night with the wind, they may cover 300 miles. Reportedly, the largest swarm studied by scientists covered 400 square miles, and was comprised of about 40 billion insects. Not very welcome invaders, to be sure!

The Jaba people of K'woi, Nigeria periodically tune in to the very loud droning of a swarm of locusts. Amazingly, the locusts' small bodies carry auditory organs on their abdomens whose volume could compete with that of an airplane engine. Farmers' heads tilt to the skies to measure the swarm's imminent arrival, and hearts fail in anticipation of the devastatingly thorough annihilation of their food supply for the next months. Though there are no railroad tracks close to K'woi, the people are aware that when a swarm of locusts descends on the tracks 35 miles away, the trains' engines are disabled, reducing the train to a sled, sliding along the slippery tracks over the bodies of thousands of locusts.

Mary Haas' years at K'woi predated the later spraying of locust swarms with concentrated insecticide solutions by airplanes, or the spreading of poisoned food among the locust bands. Rather, the farmers and their families applied the only remedy they knew how to try. They ran out to their fields with drums, tins, and other noise-makers, trying to ward off the hordes of unwelcome guests. All was in vain, except for the dubious benefit of their having caught a few locusts which they roasted over an open fire to eat as a delicacy.

At such a time of infestation, Mary went into the town to the home of the church leader, Madaki, Malam Maude. He was the head of the fledgling S.I.M. Church. She found Madaki and another elder, Paul, calmly sitting together. "Why aren't you out clanging something to chase the locusts away?" she inquired. "We decided that prayer would be much more effectual than vainly making noises which the locusts never heed, anyway," they replied. They escorted Mary to their two fields. Untouched by the locusts! Every other field in each direction was wiped clean of any sign of vegetation!

The following day was Sunday—the Lord's Day. The people gaped in astonishment as they passed the two fertile fields on their way to church, and contrasted them with their own. Never was it easier for a pastor to choose a text for a sermon—James 5:16 —"The prayer of a righteous man is powerful and effective." That visual testimony of two healthy crops, surrounded by scores of totally-consumed fields, was not soon forgotten, either by Mary or by her beloved Jabas.

It is interesting to note that the Jaba people live very close to one another, even though they are farmers. Their farms are sometimes more than ten miles away from their homes, which means that getting back and forth by foot adds an element of fatigue to their day's work. Bringing in the crop without the convenience of a truck or other vehicle is enervating. Neighbors almost always help one another with the task. One year Madaki, Malam Maude, requested that the women and girls of the congregation go to his farm, six miles away, to assist him in carrying his crop home. The next morning a large group of them answered his call, appearing with all sorts of baskets—some big, some small, some old and fragile, others new and strong. They walked together along the narrow footpath to the pastor's farm, filling the countryside with the sound of their incessant chatter and singing.

Upon reaching the farm they loaded their baskets. Some barely covered the bottom of their basket, thinking to themselves, "Why should we carry a heavy load six miles when we won't get paid for the job?" Others filled their baskets to the brim with corn, thinking with gratitude of the pastor's faithful ministry. One lady filled her big basket so full that her strength gave out before she reached the pastor's home, so she called her son to assist her the rest of the way. Her friends scolded her for taking so much, but she smiled and said, "I did it because of love for the Lord Jesus and for the pastor. I wanted to carry as much as I possibly could."

As each person arrived at the pastor's home, she was told to sit down by her basket and wait until all the others had arrived. Just at sunset the last load was carried in. It wasn't hard to see the variance in the loads carried by that circle of women. Some were overflowing, others were scant.

The pastor joined the group, thanked them all for their help, and joyously announced, "The corn you have carried on your heads those six miles is for you! You may take it home and enjoy it with your family!" None of the women had much corn left in her granary at home. Receiving an unexpected gift like that caused great excitement. The more generous carriers leaped for joy as they thanked the pastor. The others drew back, ashamed, as they picked up the meager amount of corn. "If I had only known, I would have taken a bigger basket!" moaned one as she ambled away sadly. "Another said, "I would have filled my basket if I had known it was for me!" Others asked the pastor, "Why didn't you tell us your intention? We would have brought some of our relatives along to help us!" Sadness and shame filled the hearts of the less diligent women as they learned a very practical lesson about selfishness and laziness.

Some of the women who had not responded to the pastor's request, saying that they had too much of their own work to do, heard about what had happened. Early the next morning they gathered at the pastor's house, offering to carry the rest of his corn home for him. "You are too late," he said gently. "The corn was all brought in yesterday."

The next Sunday the Pastor referred to the incident, and applied the lesson succinctly. "Many of you will be disappointed at God's harvest day. Why not start working for Him now? Fill your baskets (big ones!) with service for Him. Bring Him a harvest of souls. He will repay you with rewards far more wonderful than those the corn-carriers received from me this week!"

* * * * * * *

"Serve the Lord with gladness!"—Psalm 100:2.

"The desire of the righteous ends only in good,
but the hope of the wicked only in wrath.

"One man gives freely, yet gains even more;
another withholds unduly, but comes to poverty.

"A generous man will prosper;
he who refreshes others will himself be refreshed"
—Proverbs 11:23–25

7

Not One Penny Withheld

Respect for authority is a very important part of African culture. Being accorded a title for an accredited position elevates a person's morale exceedingly. There are innumerable nuances to the various titles, and it takes a very humble man to wear a positional title graciously. Such a man was one of the earliest converts to Christ from paganism among the Jaba people of K'woi, northern Nigeria. The title, "Madaki," means "Deputy to the Chief." It evokes respect and effuses influence, potentially for better or for worse.

Madaki Malam ("teacher") Maude was not only second in authority to the chief of the town, but he was also entrusted with the lead position in the K'woi Church which was one of the early fruits of the witness and teaching of the Sudan Interior Mission. At one time it was the largest and strongest evangelical church in the north of Nigeria. As a result of its emphasis on missionary outreach to other tribes, several of its members became the first witnesses for Christ in unreached areas, notably Kagoro which was soon to become a very large center of evangelism and church upbuilding. Pastor Toro and his family moved from K'woi to Kagoro with Mr. and Mrs. Thomas Archibald in 1927, and were to win the first of the "tailed headhunters of Kagoro" to Christ.

As Deputy Chief, Madaki Maude had served willingly without ever having received any remuneration of any kind. His advice and counsel were sought at all hours, and his people depended upon him regularly to solve daily problems.

Mr. William Watson was the first senior missionary at K'woi, and had learned of the unpaid status of Madaki Maude. In those days Nigeria was a British Colony. District Officers were in charge throughout the country, answerable to the British Governor. The visit of a D.O., as the officers were called, was always a special event to missionaries, as they seldom had contact with high officials. Houses were spotlessly cleaned, the best china was brought out for meals, children's behavior was exemplary, and the best possible impression was given. Opportunity usually ensued for chatting about the local situation.

In the course of a visit by a D.O., Mr. Watson made him aware of the fact that Madaki Maude was a faithful servant, not only to the church, but also to the Jaba people as he conscientiously carried out the duties of Deputy Chief. He also slipped in the fact that thus far Madaki Maude had never received any financial payment for his services. He did not know the reason. The District Officer was incredulous about that oversight, and made immediate note to remedy the situation as soon as he returned to his office.

The officer was as good as his word. Not long after his visit to K'woi, he mailed to Madaki Maude his very first salary for his services as Deputy Chief. The next day Madaki joyously went to see Mr. Watson, his face aglow, and his two cupped hands outstretched, obviously holding something very precious. After the usual lengthy greetings, Madaki gave Mr. Watson a wad of money. "What is this for, Malam?" asked Mr. Watson. "I just received my very first salary and I want to present it to the Lord as Firstfruits!" he replied. "The entire sum?" Mr. Watson asked. "Yes, of course, I must not withhold one penny! God deserves all! Didn't Jesus commend the widow who gave all that she had?"

If we could all learn by the power of example as the K'woi people did at that time, how blessed our churches would be! That simple, sincere dedication of Madaki's first salary to God opened the door to teach the church forthrightly the grace of giving liberally and sacrificially. The K'woi church began tithing regularly and faithfully. It is not surprising that abundant blessing followed.

> "Bring the whole tithe into the storehouse, that there may be
> food in my house. Test me in this," says the Lord Almighty,
> "and see if I will not throw open the floodgates of Heaven and
> pour out so much blessing that you will not have room
> enough for it" — Malachi 3:10.

As young Jabas increasingly went out as evangelists to neighboring tribes or villages to witness for our Lord, the missionaries at K'woi assumed the financial responsibility for their support, even though their own allowances were very small. When the Watsons retired to Scotland, Mary Haas was asked to take over the lead position at K'woi, working with Eva Doerksen. They soon realized that they could not personally finance the station upkeep and its expansion, plus the evangelists' support. Funds would not stretch that far. Providentially, Mary read a very helpful booklet entitled, "The Indigenous Church: Self-Governing, Self-Supporting, and Self-Propagating." She felt led by the Lord to share these concepts with the church elders. "Regrettably", she declared, "unless the church will assume the support of their own missionaries, we must recall them. That would surely cause the fine reputation of the church to suffer." They threw up their hands in horror at the idea of enduring such embarrassment.

The task seemed impossible. But Mary stood firm. The elders said, "No, no! Don't recall any one yet. Let us pray about the matter and we will challenge the church next Sunday with the ultimatum: **Recall, Or Support? Which?** To God's glory, the church unanimously voted to take the stupendous financial leap of faith. Growing pains increase stature!

The first year following their momentous decision, the church attendance doubled, and offerings tripled! The church continued to grow and to open new outstations. The K'woi Church's contribution to the indigenous body which grew out of the SIM's ministry, known as ECWA (The Evangelical Churches of West Africa) has been and continues to be substantial. Both in personnel and in finances, their part in the overall impact of ECWA evokes praise to God.

* * * * * * *

Paul's words to the Corinthians are appropriate:
"Now, brothers, we want you to know about the grace that God has given the Macedonian churches. Out of the most severe trial, their overflowing joy and their extreme poverty welled up in rich generosity. For I testify that they gave as much as they were able, and even beyond their ability. Entirely on their own, they urgently pleaded with us for the privilege of sharing in this service to the saints. And they did not do as we expected, but they gave themselves first to the Lord and then to us in keeping with God's will"—2 Corinthians 8:1-5.

8

No Men! No Vehicle!

"Mary! Why are you pacing off this rugged cornfield, like you're trying to measure space for a building? That's a man's job, isn't it? It's hot out here—hot enough to make you faint! Those mud bricks over there, drying in the sun, what will they be used for?"

"A man would be most welcome to take over the job, if there were one! For a long time we've had only women workers here at K'woi. Yea, I am measuring off the spot where we'll build a classroom. And yes, that line-up of drying mud bricks is part of the project."

"Is this your first such building endeavor?"

"Oh, no! This is about the thirtieth. There's the church over there, and the little dispensary building in back of you, some storerooms to your left, and a small schoolroom not far from here, and lots more. I should say that a man did come to supervise the roofing of the church building, for which we were grateful. Otherwise I've been in charge of building with the considerable help of the nationals. We've done quite a few buildings on the outstations. You're welcome to look around, but I must get this job done before darkness sets in. We don't have a long dusk period here, so excuse me while I proceed."

"But don't you need some lumber and nails and cement, etc? I haven't seen any hardware store anywhere in this area. Come to think of it, there's not even a road for a vehicle to follow to bring supplies."

"The Lord never promised all the conveniences of western civilization here, but the nationals are eager to work. They are strong, can walk long distances, and they bring my supplies, as needed. They carry them on their heads from Jos, 100 miles away. Thanks for your interest!"

Mary M. Haas was determined to finish her measuring job, so she gave her questioner no chance to detain her further. More mud bricks would be molded the next few days by the national laborers, and the carriers from Jos would arrive sometime that week. She must have the measurements all delineated. Besides, her medical clinic patients would be lined up at the dispensary in the morning, each one in a hurry to get to his farm work. But as she measured, she pondered what the Lord had allowed several single women to accomplish there at K'woi, where she was the station head. Surely the Lord knew that a man could add a lot of expertise and muscular strength to the job, and a truck could transport more lumber, but until He changed the situation, she would do what she could cheerfully and acceptably.

Even a horrible war can have some beneficial side-effects, and the need for an access road to K'woi unexpectedly opened up. Twenty-three miles from K'woi was an iron mine. One of its by-products was columbite, a black mineral compound of columbian and iron, needed urgently by the Allied Forces during World War II. It was deemed so important that the British colonists built a makeshift road right past K'woi to Kafanchan where a railroad station facilitated its transfer to Jagindi to the south. Excitement stirred the chatter between the single ladies during their meals. Said Mary one day, "I'll be going on furlough soon. Maybe the Lord will enable me to bring back a truck which will solve the supplies problem. With this new road going to Kafanchan, we can easily take the road from there directly to Jos! Let's pray about it!" And from their prayers developed a most exciting saga of God's faithfulness in meeting the needs of His dependent servants.

The war was still in progress when Mary left for her furlough, but it thankfully ended during her year at home. As the time to return to Africa drew near, the search for a truck intensified. She contacted every car agency in her area of Ohio, but met with the standard reply that no vehicles were coming off the assembly lines, except for military priorities. But tenacity in prayer continued.

Mary made a trip to Detroit, Michigan to say goodbye to Sara, her beloved sister, who was also an enterprising go-getter. Together they combed the car capital of the world, pleading for a truck. When they visited a Chrysler agency, they pitched their urgent request for a Dodge or Plymouth truck. When General Motors signs faced them, they entreated the agents for a Chevy or Olds or any other GM truck. "There's been a war, Ma'am. There are no trucks available for any one anywhere!" was the typical answer from Chrysler and G.M. The Ford dealer was then besieged with their requests for a Ford product. He mercifully breathed a ray of hope into their discouraged spirits when he said, "Miss Haas, why don't you call Henry Ford himself? See what he can do for you! If he can't help you, I don't know any one who can!" He gave Mary a telephone number to call, and she went out feeling like the proverbial choo-choo train, repeating over and over to herself, "Yes, I can! Yes, I can!" Unaccustomed as she was to phoning men of world renown, she wondered how she could quiet the excitement in her voice to state her case, though she anticipated that a large contingency of secretaries would try to block her way.

Sara and Mary went back to Sara's home, and Mary endured insistent sisterly prodding to place the call. "What have you got to lose? Dial the number! The Lord is on your side. You want the truck for His service, not for yourself! Go ahead! Place the call!"

So Mary dialed with trembling hands. A pleasant secretary answered with the polite, "May I help you?" greeting.

"I'd like to speak to Henry Ford, please," squeaked the reticent Mary.

"May I ask your name and your reason for calling, please?"

Giving her name was easy, but explaining that she, a single lady, was going back to Africa and needed a truck urgently enough to require the intervention of the world's car magnate was more difficult. But, as we say in this decade, she kept her cool.

"Just a moment, please!" Silence followed and the secretary's relaying of the message was inaudible. But, to Mary's great surprise, the secretary resumed the conversation, saying, "Kindly hold on. I'll connect you with Mr. Ford." An S.O.S. prayer zipped up to the Throne of Grace from Mary's heart as she said, "Lord, show me what to say!" In an aside to her impatient sister, Mary whispered, "I'm getting connected to Henry Ford himself!!!" Mary hoped that Sara's gasp of surprise wasn't heard on the other end. The next voice she heard said, "Miss Haas, this is Henry Ford. How may I help you?" Phew! Out flowed the story of the new road past K'woi, the many building projects for which she was responsible, the inconvenience of depending on head carriers for large amounts of supplies brought from 100 miles away, etc. The ultra-busy gentleman on the other end of the line listened attentively and sympathetically. He explained the almost impossible situation facing car manufacturers at that time, but he asked Mary to write him a letter, explaining the need for priority consideration in purchasing a truck. He gave her instructions how to address the letter to his personal attention. It was hard for Mary to thank him adequately without sounding like she was exaggerating. She felt like a leaping gazelle as she made her way to a desk and wrote the requested letter. She made sure that her home address was clearly evident.

Not too long after that exciting call, a letter from Henry Ford threatened to send her heart into fibrillation. "Miss Haas," he wrote, "I note that you live in Pandora, Ohio. We have a Ford agency in Lima, 17 miles from Pandora. I am advising Mr. Timmerman, our manager there, that we are resuming production of vehicles on a small scale, as materials become available. The first truck to arrive in Lima is to be reserved for you. I hope it reaches you on time for your return to Africa, and that it will give you good service."

Upon receiving that welcome news, Mary hastened to Lima to make initial contact with Mr. Timmerman. When she introduced herself, he said, "Miss Haas? I received a letter about you today!" Mary countered, "I am holding in my hand a letter from Mr. Ford about you!" They compared the letters. So far, so good. But then, to add dismay to joy, he showed Mary a list of 500 people whose names preceded hers, all of whom were waiting for first production vehicles. Contradicting the gloomy impact of that list, he then declared, "Yes, 500 are ahead of you, but who am I to refuse if Henry Ford himself designates the first truck to be sold to you? Be assured that I will contact you immediately when your truck is delivered!"

Shortly after that encounter, another letter from Henry Ford gave the exact date when resumption of production would begin, and the estimated date when Mary's truck would arrive in Lima. True to Mr. Ford's prediction, a few days after that estimated date, Mr. Timmerman called Mary to say that the truck had actually arrived. She should appear at the Ford agency at 2:00 p.m. that day! Mary was never one to be late for any meal or meeting or appointment, and this was to be no exception. She hustled around, readying herself for this valued acquisition. Mary's oldest sister, Clara, and her husband agreed to drive her to Lima. When they reached the Lima agency, alas, Mary was told that the appointment time had been postponed to 4:00 p.m. Window shopping can be fun sometimes, but that day it was like being on a treadmill, waiting for four o'clock.

The clock faithfully ticked away and Mary and party returned to the agency to find that Mr. Timmerman was an opportunist, first-class. Why should he simply sell a vehicle in a usual manner when he could turn the transaction into an advertising blitz? Reporters and their cameras greeted Mary. This was a big event. Every one was tired of hearing that supplies were designated for war efforts. At last, commerce for ordinary citizens could become a daily event again! And this particular sale, to some one taking an American truck to Nigeria immediately after the war, made for more than a casual story. The Lima News carried a full-page report, replete with pictures of Mr. Welty, the Sales Manager of Timmerman Motor Sales, handing over the truck keys to a delighted customer, and a woman at that! The papers of several counties surrounding Pandora also took advantage of interesting copy, to the delight of their readers. The story, in fact, has been told countless times as Mary has been begged and cajoled to tell and retell how Mr. Ford intervened on her behalf.

Mary receives the precious title for her miracle truck from Mr. Orrin S. Welty, the Sales Manager of the Lima, Ohio Ford Agency.

To a missionary, purchasing a vehicle for his ministry represents a frightening amount of money. Mary's purchase price was donated by Christian friends across the country, and was in ready cash for the big day. $800.00! A huge sum by 1945 standards! A small fraction of what such a purchase requires for today's missionary, to be sure, but a never-to-be-forgotten experience for Mary.

The cameras clicked again as petite Mary and her sister, Clara, drove away towards Pandora in a half-ton truck, followed by Clara's husband in his car. As they pulled up to the curb in front of the Haas home, family and neighbors joined in the celebration, a tangible proof that the war economy may have given way to civilian needs. Hurrah!

Immediately Mary had the back of the truck enclosed and a lockable door installed at the rear. The mission office in New York was contacted with the news, and request was made for a specific freighter booking so that the car, loaded with the rest of her belongings, could travel with her. Supplies for a four-year term of service were always considerable. Mary did not have a long wait this time. Shortly she was told to proceed to New York, bag and baggage. Her life-long friend, Fern Bixel, agreed to accompany her and help with the driving.

Mary's home church, St. John Mennonite Church of Pandora, held a dedication service for Mary and her loaded truck right after the Sunday morning service. After dinner, excitement was at a high pitch as the two women climbed into the formidable-looking truck for the long ride to New York. The goodbyes echoed in their ears for some time, and they praised God for the prayer backing they knew would follow Mary as she set off for another term of service in Nigeria. It was a new experience, driving a truck in the thick traffic of New York City, but they survived it well, and reached the mission home, only to learn that Mary's booking had been postponed. That wasn't the only postponement. Mary faced a series of departure dates, none of which materialized. One day the mission had a call saying that a new French airline had started service between Paris and Lagos, Nigeria. Did the mission have any one wishing to follow that route? So Mary, always on the ready, said, "Sure, I'd rather wait in Lagos for my car than to remain here in New York indefinitely." A booking was made for her to fly to Paris, so she drove the loaded truck to a Barber Line pier in Brooklyn, NY to await shipping to Africa.

Mary Haas at the wheel of her new Ford truck, the first off the assembly line, kindness of Henry Ford. Her friend, Fern Bixel, drove with her to New York for the first lap of her journey back to Africa.

In those post-war times, many missionaries faced bleak news when they appeared at shipping offices or airports. Mary flew to Paris and reported to the "new airline" for her ongoing booking instructions. Alas, neither the airline nor its planes had gotten off the ground. No one knew when it would be in commission. She got a taxi, and went to all the airlines which she thought might have service to Africa, trying to get a booking. To no avail. She was stranded, alone in Paris, not knowing one soul, and unable to speak French. A lady in distress, to be sure! But an American lady! And Americans have recourse to American embassies. Why not state her case there to the embassy in Paris? She made her desired destination known to the perplexed taxi driver, and soon she was facing the Paris American Embassy personnel to whom she could state her case. They escorted her to the Ambassador's office where she restated her dilemma, and he assured her that they would get her on her way. She should proceed to her hotel room, and not leave there, as they would possibly be contacting her very shortly. About 4:00 p.m. a call came through, saying that she should go to the American Transport Command immediately, which she did. She was put on a plane carrying American soldiers. As she sat down, she glanced around to find that she was the only lady on board. This chapter's title declares, "No Men!" but in this particular situation there were plenty of them, all vying for a turn to sit next to the rather gregarious Mary. But she knew that none of them would take over her job of supervising mud-brick buildings at K'woi!

At midnight they were told that they were landing at the Azores. Mary blurted out to the young man then having his turn at her side, "The Azores? I want to go to Lagos, not the Azores!" He said, "Miss Haas, we never know where we are heading! The pilot is handed a letter after the engines have started, telling him where to go, so in this case, it must have said, 'Azores.' Don't worry! You're in good hands!" Three pleasant days were spent there, being escorted around the island by the Captain's chauffeur. Then she boarded another all-male passenger transport plane which took her to Casablanca, Morocco, in the northwest corner of Africa, still a very long way from Nigeria. She was given a room in the center of a long barracks building, all by herself. Her footsteps at one end of the hallway echoed all the way to the far end. It was rather eerie! But she had soldier escorts to take her to her meals and anywhere else that she wanted to go. She spent two days there before boarding yet another transport plane which took her to Fishermen's Lake in Liberia, West Africa. She spent three weeks at the Army base, in a two-room cottage, half of which was used by the Captain's secretary. There was nothing to occupy her time, and nothing to read, except, of course, her ever-present Bible which she read faithfully. Again, she had a male serviceman as escort to every meal and was placed at the Captain's table where conversation was always pumped out of her, including the story of how she got the car which was on the high seas at that moment. One Saturday the Captain told her that the ship carrying her car was due to arrive the following week. He would take her to Monrovia to meet the ship, and, hopefully, she could board it and travel with her car to Lagos.

One day she heard that a Pan Am plane was arriving, and she went to watch the landing. She was pleasantly surprised to see three Americans disembark—two ladies and a man, and she was sure they were kindred spirits. They looked like they could be missionaries. Indeed, they were, and they were also headed for Nigeria. The single lady among them was placed in Mary's room, and she was glad for the company. The next meal she tried to include her three new friends when her escort arrived to take her to the dining room, but the escort asked, "Who are these people?" "Friends that flew in on Pan Am this morning," she replied. He said, "Sorry, but I can't take them. They belong to Pan Am, but you belong to the U.S. Army!" So Mary gave the soldier a tip, thanked him profusely, and elected to walk to the dining room with her new friends where they all sat together at the Captain's table.

True to his word, on the scheduled day the Captain took Mary to Monrovia. He and his chauffeur sat in the front while Mary was ensconced in fluffy pillows on the back seat, looking very debonair. SIM had no mission station in Liberia at that time. It wasn't until 1954 that the radio station, ELWA, was opened there, and later, ELWA Hospital and ELWA Academy for missionary children. So Mary was taken to the guest house of the Assemblies of God station. When she told the hostess that she expected to board the ship which was imminently due in port, the hostess replied, "There's no chance of that. There are only two berths open for passengers, and we already have two people here, waiting to board that ship." Mary said that she would go to the shipping office on the Monday morning to check into the matter. She bid a very grateful goodbye to the Captain and his chauffeur, and settled down to spend the weekend in a city only about 1800 miles from her final destination.

Sunday morning the two ladies and the gentleman who had been with her in Fishermen's Lake arrived, but not ensconced with pillows, nor escorted by an Army captain. They had traveled in an open truck which broke down in the pouring rain, so they were a sorry sight. Mary could not cease to be amazed at the special treatment she had received.

Monday morning the single lady who had just arrived by truck accompanied Mary to the shipping office. Mary stated her urgent need for a booking on the incoming ship, especially since her car was on it, and she would like to take possession of it in Lagos upon its arrival there. The clerk consulted the manifest and said, "You're already booked on that ship!" Incredulously, Mary asked who had placed the booking. "The captain who escorted you to Monrovia cabled out to the ship, and made the arrangements for you to board." Another intervention by the Lord on Mary's behalf! So much of what "happens" to Mary is what I term, a "Maryism." The unusual seems to be common to her experience, and all of us who know her enjoy each incident's rehearsal with her.

Innocently, Mary's voice did not mask her joy when she reported the news of her assured booking back at the A.G. Mission. The delivery of the news, understandably, met with surprise tinged with chagrin. "We've had the booking for our two workers for some time!" said the hostess.

"The shipping clerk told me that one of your ladies could go, but not both of them. I had no part whatsoever in the decision, nor was I aware that the Captain had cabled ahead on my behalf. I am very sorry for the inconvenience!" replied Mary. She was torn between her own happiness and the disappointment of these folks.

The hostess expressed her disappointment, saying, "We wouldn't consider sending one of our ladies without the other! We'll have to wait for the next opening." That enabled Mary's Fishermen's Lake roommate to board the ship with her. By that time they had become good friends.

A day or so later the ship docked and Mary and friend boarded with great anticipation of reaching Nigeria at last. Little did they know that the boat would proceed no closer to Nigeria than Takoradi in the

Gold Coast (now called Ghana). As usual, they ate their meals at the Captain's table. In the course of conversation, Mary told the Captain how she had gotten her truck which was in his baggage hold. She told him that she would like to drive to Lagos from Takoradi, if she could obtain petrol (gasoline). He said it was strictly rationed. But he offered the suggestion that Mary scurry over to the Elder-Dempster Line which had a ship leaving that night for Lagos. She should ask if they could take her and her car aboard, as well as her friend. Mary shook off her sea-legs and hurried to the office. Breathlessly, she recounted her case and to her amazement was told that if she could get the truck and herself back there within an hour's time, she could go, and her friend, as well. Mary rushed back to the Captain with the news, and he jumped into action, ordering her truck out of the hold as the first item of business. But still, no petrol! Mary noted lots of Africans hanging around, hoping for little jobs to bring them a bit of cash. So Mary summoned one of them and said hastily, "Can you get 20 men to push this truck over to the Elder-Dempster ship?" That sounded like cash to him, so he called his buddies to the task, and soon the inert truck was empowered by elbow grease, sweat, grunts and shouts. Mary and her friend sat in the front seat, and Mary steered, glancing down at her watch constantly, hoping they would not be late. They made it! The pushers got their monetary awards 'midst many chuckles, and Mary and her friend got their tickets and boarded the ship. They stood on an upper deck watching as the truck was loaded. Whoops! A rope broke, and Mary's heart almost sank to the cement pier below. But the truck reached the hold at a crooked angle and without damage! Another thing to thank the Lord for!

A two-day voyage carried them to Lagos where Mary's vehicle was off-loaded, and she made arrangements for the trip upcountry, about 800 miles. Lacking enough petrol for the entire trip, she decided to put the truck on a Nigerian Railroad car and take the train as far as Minna where she could obtain more fuel. She would go to Jos to buy the next fuel supply. It so happened that Mr. and Mrs. Bill Todd were needing a way to get to Jos, so they joined her. The truck thus began its official passenger service! Upon their eventual arrival at K'woi, the nationals were ecstatic about seeing "their car!" It was the first vehicle ever owned by any one in that area, so it was an *abin mamaki* (a thing of amazement) to all!

That truck hauled stones, cement, lumber, nails, joists, benches, grain, flour, all kinds of groceries, and people — too many to count! Whenever Mary was ready to leave for a trip, she always found a crowd gathered, hoping to be permitted to go wherever she was going. Keeping her travels a secret was an impossible task. Word of the earliest preparations for her leaving would encircle the town, and enough passengers would appear to break an axle!

The truck had no pulsating ambulance lights affixed on it, but it often served as an ambulance, dashing to deliveries of babies, snake bite victims, smallpox or meningitis epidemics, etc. One night Mary set out to take a lady who was in labor with shoulder presentation to Kafanchan Hospital, about 30 miles away. It was pouring rain, and the road was badly eroded. Elsie Hendricksen sat in the rear of the truck with the patient. The bumps and gullies caused the truck to shake constantly and unmercifully. But mercy prevailed, anyway, since the shaking undoubtedly turned the baby to the proper birth position, and soon Mary heard a tapping on the cab window and Elsie's shout, saying, "She has delivered!" Sad to say, the baby was born dead, but the mother's life was spared, for which all gave thanks as Mary turned the truck around on the narrow, muddy road, and headed back to K'woi.

The faithful Ford truck's odometer clicked up many, many miles, but Mary was never stuck on those rugged roads with it, not even once. It saw years of good service for its subsequent owner as well. The Lord's provisions are amazingly efficient, and He is worthy of praise for supplying every need.

9

A Skull-Rattling Night

Mary had heard about the Yeskwa tribe, located about 20 miles west of K'woi. Reputedly, the Yeskwas were totally unreached by the Gospel, living in primitive conditions, practicing animism. One day in the forties she packed her trekking gear—camp cot, washbasin, cooking pot, kerosene lamp, and a small amount of food, and started out to visit the Yeskwas. A local evangelist agreed to accompany her over the rough roads. They would have to walk, encountering thick foliage, rocks and ridges, streams, and possibly snakes and biting insects.

Twenty wearying miles had sapped their strength by the time they reached the outskirts of the Yeskwa tribe's jealously-protected area. No white person had ever invaded their privacy before, much less a white woman! Village elders intercepted Mary's trudge into sacrosanct territory. They were unresponsive to her claims of fatigue, and pleas for one night's hospitality. They pointed beyond their borders, advising Mary to keep moving. But her persuasive powers forced the elders to meet in seclusion to discuss this unprecedented event. They emerged, looking uncannily triumphant, and even a speck hospitable. Word of their dilemma had spread throughout the town, so there were many witnesses to the voicing of the decision to allow Mary to sleep in the "juju hut." it was surely not a pleasant prospect to enter the spirit-worship center, but Mary was ready to drop almost anywhere. She thanked her erstwhile hosts.

She and her cot barely squeezed into the low, narrow entrance to the small grass hut. Alas, the cot had to rest over a hole through which food was dropped down daily to a corpse, buried below. Above the cot, under the grass roof, was a ledge bearing quite a few skulls. Of humans, or of monkeys, she did not know. Courage, Mary, courage! She innocently settled down, entrusting herself to the Lord's faithful watch care. She shut her eyes. What she didn't see or know would not hurt her. Darkness hid the skulls.

All night long the shelved skulls above her and the bones below her were rattling and shaking as rats scavenged for food. Dawn could not come fast enough for this initiate to the eerie world of animism. When it did, Mary crawled outside and set up her basin to wash off the dust of her previous day's journey. Fatigue had precluded worrying about hygiene the night before. In the very dim light of dawn she knew she was not alone. A furtive glance around her revealed scores of slinking bodies and beady eyes. Hunched against surrounding huts and trees, Yeskwas watched her every move with bated breath.

After a short while the elders addressed the cringing crowd. "Come out in the open, all of you! We want this white woman to reveal her big secret to every one. We had been sure that the spirits whom we worship would kill her during the night. But see for yourselves, she has survived! Her Spirit must be stronger than our spirits. Listen carefully to what she says."

Mary was never one to avoid a God-given opportunity to witness to the love, grace, and power of her Lord and His great salvation. Her soul was in her message, which was interpreted from the Jaba language which Mary had learned to the Yeskwa tongue. She had a captive audience. Her evangelist also gave a fervent explanation of the Gospel of Christ. He and Mary could leave the village that day with a much lighter burden. The trip home seemed shorter. Mission accomplished (or, perhaps, just begun!)

Several months later a delegation appeared at K'woi, asking that a teacher be sent to Yeskwa to tell the people more about the Lord. The delegates saw the K'woi Bible School, and though they were illiterate, they decided to enroll shortly thereafter. Eventually they became the resident evangelists to the Yeskwas, greatly extending the impact of Mary's visit. Mary rejoiced in having been permitted to live out Paul's admonition to Timothy:

> *"The things you have heard me say in the presence of many witnesses entrust to reliable men who will also be qualified to teach others"*—2 Timothy 2:2.

S.I.M. was often jokingly called by missionaries the "Sure, I'll Move" mission. When Council members met to discuss filling vacancies on stations, starting new projects, etc., missionaries held on to their jobs tentatively. So, in the course of time, Mary was transferred to another station, and did not hear anything further about developments at Yeskwa. In 1968, after 43 years of service, she "retired" to the U.S.A.

About two years after Mary left Nigeria her former co-worker, Elsie Hendricksen, was preparing to retire to Canada. Elsie, wanting to send Mary a report, visited Yeskwa to see if the seed sown by Mary and the Bible School graduates had borne fruit. To Elsie's amazement, a very adequate church building graced the center of Yeskwa town. Every villager was regularly attending the Sunday services and Bible classes, and a school had been erected for the children.

When Mary had visited Yeskwa in the early forties, she encountered the tribe's custom involving the birth of a baby girl. The first man, regardless of his age or character, who brought a pot of water to a new mother was promised ownership of the child following its having been weaned. The little girl's work included keeping her owner's pipe lit. She would place embers from a fire into the pipe, puff heavily on it, and then turn it over to the man. As a result, every man, woman, and child in the village was addicted to tobacco. What a contrast Elsie saw in 1970! Not a puff of tobacco smoke was visible. The pipes had been discarded, all without any cajoling from missionaries. The people were clothed, and the "juju hut" was nowhere to be seen. The rats were, no doubt, alive, but they had to search elsewhere for bones to rattle.

10

Maryisms

Admittedly, the title of this chapter will not be defined in any reputable dictionary. It is a word, conveniently-coined to denote the frequent occurrences of the unusual in Mary Haas' life. I make no claim to having covered all of them. I often say, "Why haven't I listed that among the "Maryisms?" No doubt, the reader will, or has already met up with the unusual in other chapters of this book, such as Mary's "Queen for a Day" experience.

One of my first personal impressions of the fact that Mary's extraordinary experiences really do occur was when she and I had finalized all of the meticulous planning to embark on a Templeton Boat Cruise, featuring Dr. Charles Stanley as the speaker. Our day of departure was imminent. But so was an angina attack. Consulting my cardiologist, I was informed that instead of going cruising, I was flying to Florida Hospital in Orlando for another Angiogram and Angioplasty. I called the Templeton Tours and got instructions about how to get a refund by submitting a doctor's advice. I asked if they had a waiting list, or whether I should try to get some one to buy my ticket. The Tours operator said not to worry. They would assign our lower deck cabin to a couple listed on the waiting list, and Mary would be privileged to enjoy a First Class top deck cabin with many amenities in the nicest section of the boat, if she agreed. She was listening to the conversation and agreed readily! The rest is easy to imagine. She was treated royally throughout the trip, and I dreamed of trying again another year. (I did go several years later).

As Mary and I go together on frequent shopping errands, it is not unusual for some gentleman to approach Mary politely and ask her what she does to her hair, as it is such a gorgeously pure white. "I wish my wife's hair looked like yours," one vendor said wistfully. I shuffle along behind, wishing that mine were not a steel grey! No one needs to inquire how I made it that way.

Quite a few years ago Mary's sister, Sara, made a decision not to travel by plane anymore. She drives in Los Angeles traffic daily, but no matter how urgently we wish she would visit us here, her mind is made up to stay on terra firma. But a few years ago she and Mary made a plane trip together. They were in the process of changing planes at Atlanta when an official directed all of the passengers into a central room. He told them to go to the bus parked in a certain place, but he isolated Mary and Sara, saying, "You two sisters with the white hair, follow me!" They followed, wondering if it was for good or for ill, and also wondering how he knew they were sisters. He escorted them to a long, shining limousine. The official addressed the

Two white-haired sisters, Sara and Mary, on Mary's 80th birthday.

chauffeur, saying, "Take these women to the plane for flight number so-and-so, and help them with their baggage until they are settled on the plane." The chauffeur followed the instructions well, and they settled into their assigned seats comfortably, well ahead of the other passengers. When they arrived, they said to Mary and Sara, "You must be some sort of celebrities to get special treatment like that!" Well, all children of God are special, but not all reflect the fact that "the King's daughters are all glorious within!"

During Mary's earliest introduction to life in Africa, she had the unexpected tutelage of a dear Scottish lady, Mrs. Allen. All of the resident missionaries of Kurmin Musa ate together. Mary had been brought up strictly to eat what was placed in front of her without fussing, and that training has stuck with her for 95 years. However, in 1925, getting accustomed to many new tastes and new smells all at once was quite a chore. One day okra was served. Mary gingerly tasted the seemingly slimy green vegetable, and decided that it was not for her. Mrs. Allen didn't miss a trick. She said emphatically, "Mary, you must eat the okra! It is the only green we have, and it is rich in iron. It's good for you!" Mary demurred. Obeying a senior missionary was a cardinal virtue. She must learn to eat it. Learn she did, and ever since that time she has loved it. In fact, if I see it on the grocery shelf and want to bring Mary a treat, I buy her some okra once in a while!

When Mary was in New York at the Mission Home, preparing to embark on another term, she went shopping. Mrs. Trout, the beloved matron of the Home, inquired about what Mary had bought that day. Mary innocently said, "Bobby socks." Little did Mary know that ankle socks were a "no-no" in Mrs. Trout's eyes. She was a motherly person with an unlimited measure of love for appointees and missionaries. But every one should be allowed at least one quirk, and still be loved. Socks were her quirk. She considered them as beneath the dignity of missionaries. She quivered as she said to Mary, "I'm afraid we can't let you return to Africa." Mary was speechless. She had not submitted her life to Africa for a short period of time. It was a career commitment that she had made, and she expected to continue the work which the Lord had begun through her. She did more praying than sleeping that night. The next day Mrs. Trout consulted Dr. Rowland Bingham, the founder and General Director of the SIM. He looked gruff, but his looks belied a tender heart, and a flexible mind. He said, "Mrs. Trout, I don't think we can allow some bobby socks to keep a fine missionary from her calling and her work. Let her go!" So Mary proceeded on her way to continue her illustrious career, bobby socks in her baggage, but even more importantly, the seal of approval of the Director on her ministry.

Twice every year the Field Council met to discuss stationing of workers, problems arising, etc. One time, shortly before they were to meet, a Mrs. Smith of the Church Missionary Society of England gave a message at our Miango Rest Home about the need to organize a fellowship for church women. So SIM Council discussed the matter and decided to ask Mary Haas and Effie Varley of Miango to travel throughout Nigeria to present the idea to the women. They chose Mary and Effie because the largest groups of women in the SIM were at their respective stations, K'woi and Miango. Mary and Effie traveled in Mary's truck for one month, covering every SIM station in Nigeria. They were not permitted to enter Niger at that time. They met with enthusiastic response from the church women and the missionaries. The name in Hausa became *Zumuntar Mata*, the women's fellowship. It has been a very dynamic force within the entire Christian community, not only in SIM churches, but in all of the denominations. The women display remarkable love for one another in practical ministries. They are zealous evangelists, but also capable social workers, carrying wood or water or food to new mothers or to the ill, visiting the grief-stricken, supporting their own evangelists within the Evangelical Missionary Society, (the missionary arm of the Evangelical Churches of West Africa. ECWA is the large church body mothered to maturity by the S.I.M.) The women's organization gives their local pastors spiritual, financial, and moral support. There have been efforts to start a similar fellowship for men, but nothing comparable to the massive *Zumuntar Mata* has emerged. (Almost every American church has its Women's Missionary Society, but not many can boast of having a Men's Missionary Society!).

The women love to wear identical stylish head cloths, blouses, and wraparound skirts, and take advantage of every opportunity to give public witness to their solidarity. Once a year the fellowships all meet together for a huge conference for Bible teaching and inspiration. That trip around Nigeria by Mary and Effie has borne fruit a million fold!

Eva Doerksen, one of Mary Haas' co-workers at K'woi, had a parrot, predictably called, "Polly." She was treated almost like a human by the nationals. Every one knew Polly on a first-name basis. Eva wrote a book of short spiritual applications from incidents involving Polly. That book went through many editions. When Eva left K'woi for an assignment in Jos, the Nigeria Headquarters, she gave Mary Haas her treasured parrot, as it did not seem kind to take her to the city. Polly stood on her perch as a welcoming sentinel on Mary's porch. She knew Mary's Jaba name well. In fact, too well! One day at rest hour Mary heard her name being called very distinctly, *"Tiri K'woi!"* (daughter of K'woi). Mary nestled deeper into her pillow, telling herself that she had made it clear to the people around that that hour must be guarded for her mid-day rest period. They must not disturb her then. They knew full well that she was available throughout the rest of the day. But the calls became more and more insistent. Finally, she tossed the pillow off her head and went to the door, but found no one there. That action was repeated several times when she finally turned to Polly and said, "Was that you, calling me?" The porch resounded for a full fifteen minutes with the heartiest deep laughter that any parrot could emit. Funny now, but that day it wasn't funny. So much for that rest hour! For most of us, having our name called by a parrot would be unusual. For Mary? No!

One day Polly flew off the porch. Distress spread among all the nationals, as well as among the missionaries. Polly was too good a friend to lose. Ruth Veenker dismissed the children from school to spread themselves around the town, looking for Polly. Alas! A hawk must have found a colorful prey. Polly was never seen again, but she's still vivid in many memories. The nationals came to Mary to mourn her loss, almost as though Polly were human.

One of our greatest surprises when we get to Heaven may be the revelations of multiple interventions in our lives of which we were totally unaware. Some of us probably keep our guardian angels very busy. Mary's little scooter seems like an exceedingly poor defense against a large herd of huge African elephants! She was travelling happily along the rough bush roads which connected her station, K'woi, with a station called Diko, about 50 miles away, She was absolutely unaware of any danger whatever. But just as she met up with a young Fulani herdsman, leading his father's cattle home, she noticed that a great many trees had been totally uprooted and thrown to the ground. The young man was astounded that she had not heard the clamor of the heavy hoofs and the thuds of the trees as they were felled. He was still shaking with fear. Only seconds before Mary had approached that area the lumbering beasts had gone through the woods, destroying everything. It makes one shudder to think of how she would have been trampled to death had she arrived even moments beforehand.

> *"You, O Lord, keep my lamp burning;*
> *my God turns my darkness into light.*
> *With your help I can advance against a troop;*
> *with my God I can scale a wall.*
> *As for God, His way is perfect;*
> *the word of the Lord is flawless.*
> *He is a shield*
> *for all who take refuge in him.*
> *For who is God besides the Lord?*
> *And who is the Rock except our God?*
> *It is God who arms me with strength*
> *and makes my way perfect"* — Psalm 18:28-33

By 1948 Mary had been in the K'woi area for 23 years. The work load had become heavier and heavier. She had supervised the erection of many buildings, but with each such project she became more aware that a man was needed at that all-ladies' station. The

"Maryism" in this incident concerns the fact that the SIM Council gave Mary the privilege of choosing her own successor, rather than having them assign someone to a situation which they could not possibly know as well as Mary did. Mary chose Ray and Lois Veenker who had worked in the Sokoto area of northwest Nigeria among Muslims. Ray had visited his sister, Ruth, at K'woi a few times. Thus Mary had been able to assess his suitability to the K'woi situation, which was entirely different from his previous one. Everyone who knows the splendid work which Ray and Lois did at K'woi is sure that the choice was not only Mary's, but the Lord's. Ray and Lois have been especially close to Mary ever since. They have been of inestimable blessing here at Sebring, and at camps and nursing homes where they have served during summer trips northward. On May 27, 1997 Ray heard the ultimate higher call. Several days after his beautiful memorial service and burial, Lois found a note in his Bible written by his own hand, saying, "As I now enter into the presence of the Lord, my hope has been fulfilled. You who remain are still hopeful. I have attained, and joyfully await your arrival in the glory of the Lord whom we endeavor to serve faithfully. R.V."

Ray's promotion is clearly a case of a Christian's "gain" which leaves a huge gap in the closely-knit fellowship of a Christian community. He had exercised his "gift of helps" generously, making a big difference in many lives. He was an expert at woodworking, especially in making grandfather clocks for family and friends. His last job, put in place just days before he went to Heaven, was in constructing a beautiful mailbox rack, with a cubbyhole for every resident, and room for new residents as they arrive. It is being enjoyed daily with amazement that he was enabled to finish and install it, as only he could. We are left to thank His Lord and ours for the privilege of having known and loved Ray Veenker.

To Mary Haas, Ray was like a brother. She fittingly sat as an esteemed member of the family at the memorial service. She is drawing upon God's grace, as are his beloved Lois and their four daughters and their families, in order to appreciate the splendor he now enjoys in Glory.

We've all heard of "under-the-table" shady deals. Mary, of all people, was involved in an "under-the-table" incident, but it wasn't shady! As was described above, she was given the privilege of choosing her successor at K'woi. That choice had a sequel. She was asked, as well, where she would prefer to go for her next assignment. She replied that she would prefer to be involved with a newer work rather than an established ministry. The Council met and discussed Mary's relocation. While they were writing a short list of places for her consideration, Mr. Cyril Forth quickly scribbled his bright idea on a piece of paper which he folded and passed under the table to the presiding officer. It read, "Send Mary Haas to Rinjin Gani, please!" Problem solved! All agreed, and so did Mary. For 20 years she enriched the history of that station. Her fellowship with Cyril and his lovely wife, Lillian, was always pleasant. Mr. Harold Hide soon joined them, and later brought his bride, Elma, to Rinji. They, too, became valued partners. The Lord had many nationals in that area for Mary to love and draw to Him. The end of chapter 12 describes two of them.

On a very different subject, how many of us can say that we were presented with the gift of a two-week-vacation at a beautiful motel on Sanabel Island, Florida? Not Many! But Mary was! Years ago a Christian motel owner with connections with some SIM personnel phoned Dick Brandt, then Manager at our Sebring Retirement Village. He asked if Dick knew any of our residents who might like to enjoy, absolutely free of charge, a two-week vacation by the ocean. Not surprisingly, Dick singled out the adventurous Mary Haas who was always eager to be on the go. Mary jumped at the opportunity, and asked Sadie Hay if she would like to accompany her. Sadie packed her case, too, and both revelled in the beauty of the sea for that unexpected vacation. Missions is supposedly full of sacrifices, but the Lord sees to it that even earthly compensations come our way. The Lord said that the awards come, "in this life and in the life to come." God is no man's debtor. What a privilege it is to serve Him!

Much more recently, in November of 1995, Mary was singled out for a very special treat. The entire SIM Retirement Village in Sebring is honored every Thanksgiving time with the visit of a Sunday School class from Douglas, Georgia, taught by Travis MacDonald, a former SIM missionary to the Sudan. They bring a completely-prepared dinner, poinsettias for the festive table, a two-pound bag of cracked pecans for each resident, and a small gift for each person. The occasion is a highlight of the year as those delightful people share their love and service with us. They have similar projects elsewhere throughout the year as well. Mr. and Mrs. Travis MacDonald head the group, and drive the van that carries the emissaries of cheer and bounty. As the tables were being cleared after the sumptuous feast of '95, Mary Haas was approached by Mr. MacDonald and asked if she would Like to accompany their group, along with Dorris Motley, one of our residents, to Douglas for a four day visit to their church. "Go! Go!" was always Mary's response. Her small case was packed within minutes and she was off with the church group.

Such southern hospitality as Mary enjoyed was the subject of many conversations after her return. Her charm and vigor were immediate hits in Douglas. Within that short space of time she was invited to speak to the Sunday School class which always sponsors our Thanksgiving dinner, to a group at a Nursing Home, and to two groups gathered in homes. It's one thing to be chosen for some special favor, but quite another to make sure that the blessing you provide is commensurate with that proffered. Mary didn't fail on that score. She has been invited to return again. The MacDonalds insisted on taking Dorris and Mary back to Sebring as well—another seven-hour trip. They loaded the van for the return trip with clothing for our Boutique, and villagers are still sporting those items.

At a retirement center many milestones are celebrated with various degrees of intensity. Some come and go, almost unnoticed. But in 1991, as Mary's 90th birthday approached, Lois Veenker, Helen Vetter and I got together to plan a big celebration which would include the entire village, plus a few outside church or ministry associates of Mary. Very special decorations were hung or placed on the tables, several huge cakes were ordered, all kinds of cookies and other goodies were prepared, a "newspaper" clipping screaming, "Mary Haas hits 90!" was posted on the bulletin board, and more than a hundred congratulatory cards were placed in baskets as the guests arrived. Ray Veenker was the inveterate Emcee, prepared with humorous anecdotes about Mary. Tributes were given by a number of close friends, and Mary was given an opportunity to tell one of her famous stories to her captive audience. All was recorded on a videotape by one of our nurses.

To top off the 90th birthday celebration, the Veenkers asked Mary what she would like for her birthday. She blurted out her long-entertained wish. "I want to go deep-sea fishing!" Veenkers were always

Travis MacDonald and his Sunday School class brought a post-Thanksgiving dinner from Douglas, GA for all the SIM village residents.
MacDonalds and their crew, ready to serve us a delicious dinner.

90th birthdays are extra-special! This one got into print, kindness of Gladys Huyler.

Right:Mary admires her cake while Belva Overmiller cuts it.

Christmas and birthday decorations blended well. Mary enjoys the goodies. Evelyn Davis at left.

Ray and Lois Veenker treated Mary to a deep-sea fishing cruise for her 90th.
Mary caught a big one!

ready for anything, but the weather was not ready for Mary's request. It was held in abeyance until April when Mary and I went with the Veenkers to a place on Florida's west coast where we boarded a fishing vessel for an exciting day on the Gulf of Mexico. Mary kept the captain busy, taking her fish off her line. A group of Canadian tourists told Mary that they had no place to cook their catch, so they would add theirs to hers. Mary loves fish, but I only like to catch them, not eat them. Ray cleaned them for her, she froze them, and ate them when I wasn't with her.

Mary is quick to give the Lord all the glory for her blessings, including her longevity. She says, "We constantly use addition when figuring our age or the sequence of events, but the Lord prefers the multiplication tables." The Scripture says that 'the blessing of the Lord brings wealth, and He adds no trouble to it' (Proverbs 10:22). It also says that He who ministers seed to the sower, multiplies the seed sown (2 Corinthians 9:10). Her reaching that memorable 90th birthday enabled her to share her testimony to God's faithfulness in multiplying the Seed which she was privileged to sow in many places. That occasion has to be counted among the very special "Maryisms" which characterize the life of this friend who is dear to all who know her. Her friends regret that no similar celebration was held for her 95th birthday, though a group of about 15 of us treated her to a birthday dinner at a local restaurant. We have our sights set on the 100th, unless the Lord returns before then, or clothes us with immortality by His triumph over death.

Let us go back in time to about 1947. Mary was teaching some African children about the calendar. It was December 31st, and she showed the children that that is the last day of the calendar year. She added, "That's my birthday, too!" One bright-eyed learner called out, "Mama, you almost weren't born!" The Lord foreknew that Mary would be of blessing to many people, so He gave her good family background, excellent health, a splendid appetite, happy associations in ministry, an intense love of hospitality, a keen sense of humor, an enriching devotional life, loyalty to the tenets of the Word of God, and an unmitigated love for people and for her Lord. There is cause for rejoicing that Mary Haas was born! Whether we know Mary personally, or only through this book, we are impressed by the grace of God, working within the life of a woman who loves Him with all her heart, soul, and mind.

11

African "Queen" Becomes a USA "Queen for a Day"

In 1961 Mary M. Haas was on furlough from her missionary work in Nigeria under the Sudan Interior Mission. At K'woi her name in the Jaba (tribal) language was *Tiri K'woi*. In the Hausa language, used very extensively by many tribes for inter-communication and market trading, she was known as *Sarauniya*, meaning "queen." At Rinjin Gani she worked entirely either in Hausa or in English. So her name, "Queen" was heard constantly.

Her brother's home in Pandora, Ohio was her furlough base. As the time for her return to Africa drew near, she traveled to Long Beach, California to visit her sister, Sara Francis. Sara is Mary's junior by two years. They share the same ebullient nature—always jovial, frequently ready for new adventures. One morning Sara announced to Mary that she "felt psychic." (Not really!) "Let's call my four friends and attend the program that Jack Bailey emcees, 'Queen for a Day'. I have a strong feeling that you'll be picked to be a contestant." Mary, very suspicious of the unfamiliar possibility of Sara's being "psychic" put up a mild fuss, and protested that she wouldn't stand a chance of being selected. But before too long the six amused ladies found themselves standing in a line two blocks long, outside the NBC studio from which the very popular daily program, "Queen for a Day" would be aired nationwide.

Shortly after their arrival, a gentleman passed out a piece of paper to each woman in line, asking that she write her name, address, occupation, and the award which she would prefer to receive in the event that she would be chosen as the queen for that day. Considerable hemming and hawing was heard among the women, but Mary knew what her urgent needs were. She quickly wrote, "A thousand-watt generator and a mimeograph for my missionary work in Nigeria, West Africa." She feared that her suggestions would not sound glamorous-enough to be given a second glance by the judges.

Eventually the signal was given for all the hopefuls to file into the scene of the dinner show. They submitted their papers as they entered, and started to enjoy their meal. As they ate, the judges chose twenty papers from among the several hundred received. They called up to the front the twenty ladies who had written them; Mary among the twenty! They were asked to relate why they had made those particular choices. Four women were then picked to be finalists, and Mary's was the fourth name called out. Jack Bailey interviewed every one of the four. The audience's reaction to each presentation would be determined by an applause meter. The first lady said that she needed a home helper for the two weeks following the imminent birth of her expected twin babies. The applause was moderately hopeful. Lady number two said that she gained her livelihood by ironing shirts, and she needed a new steam iron. Good idea, but the meter was less than ecstatic. The third contestant said that she wanted a bicycle for her neighbor's young son, since his had been stolen. He would be overjoyed to have a replacement. An unselfish request, but, alas, the meter exercised little spontaneity.

Then came Mary's turn! Jack said, "I see you are a missionary, and obviously a very happy one." to which Mary replied, "Yes, I wouldn't exchange jobs with anyone!" He proceeded with the interview, saying, "I note that you care for 600 leprosy patients in Africa, you teach the Bible in the schools, and your remote village is cut off from electrical services. What would you like to have?" Sara and her friends were threatening to have a case of apoplexy by this time as they watched and waited for Mary to activate that applause meter. Mary answered with surprising self-control that she had two requests! First, a one-thousand-watt generator would bring light to her house and to the compound church and school buildings, and to her coworkers' house. It would be a transforming acquisition! Secondly, she constantly faced tedious work in preparing notes for her Bible studies. A mimeograph would be put to optimum use. Jack asked Mary quite a few questions about Africa, her living quarters and her work. Then he proclaimed to the audience, "Here is a missionary that wants to be lit up!"

The applause meter sprang into action, the needle trembling at the end of the spectrum with no way to go further. No doubt, Sara and her friends had sore hands for a few days. Jack pronounced Mary to be the Queen for the Day. The studio went wild as a glittering crown was placed on her head and an ermine jacket put around her shoulders. The cameras flashed! Jack then read a list of all the bonus gifts, contributed by various corporations, which would be Mary's, in addition to her two practical requests. With great excitement Sara and her four friends called their husbands to come to Hollywood, and they would all take Mary out to a Chinese Restaurant for her first queenly meal. Laughter and chatter took precedence over the food!

The crowning moment! Jack Bailey and assistant seemed to enjoy their task.
photo: R. Widman

The next day an assigned host appeared at Sara's house to escort Mary and Sara to a beauty parlor for Mary's fancy hairdo and the first and last professional manicure of her lifetime. Then he took the ladies to the "Brown Derby," at that time one of Hollywood's most prestigious restaurants. Excitement blurred the menu, and both of them ordered hamburgers! They were assigned a five-room suite in a luxurious hotel, to be theirs for 24 hours. They were treated to a scrumptious meal that evening—shrimp cocktail and all. The schedule called for them to attend a Hollywood extravaganza, but Mary declined to accept that, preferring Sara's suggestion that they go to see a Lowell Thomas Travelogue which they enjoyed.

The following day many details about the dispatch of all the awards consumed a lot of time. Since Mary was due to return to Nigeria before long, rush orders had to be placed upon most items. The original plan to ship them directly to Africa failed, so they shipped them to Mary's brother's home. Pandora is a small community, rarely the scene of a TV celebrity's appearance. Every one knew Mary, so news of the upcoming airing of the "Queen for a Day" program spread like wildfire. Jack Bailey had notified the local paper about the specific date of the TV program. Mary was still away from home and would watch the program in a hotel lobby across from the Moody Bible Institute of Chicago where she was attending the annual "Founder's Week" Conference. But NBC-TV reigned uncontested in Pandora that day. The High School as well as the Elementary School students went to their assembly halls to watch the program. The Pandora Bank closed long enough to allow its employees to see their town "put on the map" by one of their well-known villagers. The Ladies' Aid Societies of the churches in Pandora postponed their monthly meetings by one day so that the members would not be denied the fun of watching Mary's having conquered the applause meter, far away in California.

When Mary returned home, she found that a number of the gifts had begun to arrive at the Funeral Home of which her brother, Milford, was the proprietor. Friends besieged her with calls daily, asking, "What arrived today?" Mary soon realized that she must share the sight of all this bounty with the town folks. She asked Milford if she could hold an open house before she packed everything for shipping to Nigeria. He said, "Yes—if we don't have a funeral that day!" Well, even the dying cooperated, and 150 people climbed the funeral home steps to the room above where all the beautiful gifts were displayed.

A few minor miracles ensued, bringing everything to Pandora on time for her departure, except for the four-poster canopy bed which was shipped shortly afterwards. At her retirement from Africa in 1968 the 4-poster followed her to Sebring, Florida, and she still nestles into it every night. At the last report (1996) the diesel generator was still in constant use in the village where Mary had ministered. Her gifts included: 24 bed sheets and pillowcases (which she donated to the Mission Hospital in Africa), a beautiful 48-piece set of Fiesta crystal glasses, goblets, plates, and dessert dishes, (most of which she still uses), a lovely table and six matching chairs (still intact and in constant use in a rest facility in Africa), the bed, a washer and dryer, kitchen appliances, dresses, blouses, hosiery, a wristwatch with two gleaming diamonds, and costume jewelry. What a windfall for any woman! More than fit for a missionary "queen!"

Mary is constantly asked to relate this story to guests who frequent her small apartment in the SIM Missionary Retirement Village of Sebring, Florida. Her enthusiasm never wanes. Her gratitude for the gifts increases with the years. The heads of the contributing corporations informed Jack Bailey that Mary Haas was the first winning contestant on the program who ever took the time and effort to write a separate expression of thanks for each particular gift. Mr. Bailey mentioned that fact during the airing of the program which occurred several months after the original taping.

The bedroom houses the "Queen for a Day" bed.

Mary still uses the crystal goblets received as "Queen for a Day."

Mary was that program's queen for just one day, but in the hearts of her myriad friends she remains a queen forever. At this writing, she is only a few months away from her 96th birthday. Those who know her best have difficulty keeping up with her zest for life and service to the Lord who called her to be His own. This incident is but one in a long list of what I call, " Maryisms." (See Chapter 10). Wherever she goes and whatever she does, something delightfully surprising occurs. May it ever be so until the greatest delight of all confronts her, and she will bow and cast all her crowns before the Lord whom she adores, and whom she has served faithfully since she was 23 years old. She has left her mark on many lives, including my own. I enjoy the privilege of being her companion as we share meals and travel together, and encourage one another in facing the encroaching limitations of increasing age.

12

Mary, a Favorite with Children

Mary Haas' personality seems to abound in built-in magnets which draw children to her instinctively. When my grandchildren visit me, quite a few times a day they slip away to Mary's apartment where a great deal of giggling and game-playing take place. When I go to visit them, one of their first questions is, "How is Aunt Mary?" When I'm heading home again, I hear, "Be sure to greet Aunt Mary for me. Tell her I love her!"

During the summer of 1996 Mary was experiencing trouble with one of her eyes. The loving SIM village nurses suggested that she cover the sore eye with a black patch to keep out the light. Mary did not let that hinder her from making her daily rounds of the village on her electric scooter. She was riding along the path when she came upon one of Bill and Velma Neef's grandsons, here in Sebring for a brief visit. She stopped to say "Hi!" to the little fellow, who was immediately enamored of the black patch. It looked like what he had seen in some of his story books. "Are you a pirate?" he asked, incredulously. Mary assured the tyke that, though she might look like one, she was perfectly harmless. She asked, "How would you like to have a ride with me on my scooter?" "Yeh! I'd like that," he replied, climbing aboard with alacrity. They took a spin around the circle and she let him steer the scooter a bit, and then she let him help her enter the apartment complex where she lives. "We park the scooter right here in the hall," she said. He dismounted and quickly disappeared to report his exploits to his Mom and to his wide-eyed twin brother. The next day Mary met Grandma Neef (now with the Lord) and told her about her enjoyment of her grandson who thought she was a pirate. Problem solved for the Neefs! The little scooter rider had been talking incessantly about "Auntie Pirate." and they could not imagine whom he was talking about! It was Mary, always a lover of children, but now wearing a title as pirate of the village. Thankfully, the eye-patch has long been put away, but the nomenclature arises frequently as Mary describes her venture as a one-eyed pirate.

Grandchildren are among the most warmly welcomed visitors to Sebring. Many of the single "aunties" know them by name, and treat them as special. One of the Veenkers' grandsons, Josh, makes a "bee line" to Mary Haas' home every time he visits his grandparents. One day he dashed into "Aunt" Mary's house with the look of some one trying to figure out a profound problem. Without too much ado, he faced Mary and said, "I have an awful taste in my mouth!" It takes a discerning auntie to solve anything as difficult as that! Mary had experience in following a child's glance around a room in order to decipher his intentions. This day as she followed the direction of his eyes, sure enough, they were fastened on the candy dish across the room. "Do you think a piece of candy might possibly help to take care of that, Josh?" she asked. "Oh, yes, I'm sure it would!" And it did. She rarely lacks a dish of candy on her table near the window, because the contents just might solve some more ponderous problems.

To return to tales of Africa in the forties, Mary's schedule as head of the station and of the clinic at K'woi in northern Nigeria was full, to say the least. But she loved to teach children as often as possible. She was able to go to the Government school to teach occasionally in after-school hours, reaching children who were not otherwise exposed to the Gospel message. When, in 1948 she was transferred to Rinjin Gani, she tried to get similar openings, but did not have the required permission. Her love of children was not to be shelved or denied.

Her reputation as a gracious hostess and a fine cook followed her to Rinji, as the station was most often called. Fellow-missionaries and other expatriates, as well, were glad to accept her hospitality. "Expatriates" was the term given to foreigners, that is, those not born in Nigeria, but residing there. Two British couples, the John Clarks and the Bill Barlows, were invited to her home fairly often. If too long a time elapsed between their visits, they would appear and say, "Isn't it about time, Mary, for us to taste a delicious 'Better Homes & Gardens' meal?" She would set a date, and happy fellowship would ensue as they enjoyed American cooking.

One time they had an outdoor pig-roast. Evidently it was their custom to put an apple in the pig's mouth for the roasting-time, but since apples were nowhere to be found in Nigeria, they put an orange between the victim's teeth. That meat defied description. Even now Mary drools as she talks about it.

As the Easter season was drawing near one year, the Clarks were Mary's guests. Instead of centering their talk around their jobs as teachers in the Government Teacher Training School, as they usually did, the Clarks were concentrating on a personal problem. They had three children, two of whom they had been forced to leave in the U.K. for their schooling. They wanted desperately to go home for Easter holidays to be with them. But the third child, a younger son who lived with them in Nigeria, was ill with a serious case of epilepsy. The doctor discouraged the idea of taking him home to England and back within a short period of time. The trip might be too stressful for him. The parents were bemoaning their situation, wanting to go, but needing to stay, because the child could not be left alone.

Mary listened to the sad story, and then gently proposed a solution which she really did not think they would accept. "If you would entrust your son to my care for the two weeks of your absence, and if you would not hold me responsible should he become seriously ill, I would be happy to care for him." The Clarks jumped at the idea. "There is no one we could trust more than you, Mary! That would be wonderful! Our children in England would be so very grateful!" They proceeded then to outline all the things that could happen, should one of their son's serious seizures occur; how Mary could contact them; even to the unthinkable details of what she should do if he suffered a fatal seizure!

Plans fell into place rapidly. The Clarks departed, and Mary's adopted "son" came to live with her. She set up a cot right beside her bed which could fit under her mosquito netting so that she could watch him, waking or sleeping. She fed him well with all kinds of treats. He escorted her everywhere she went—to the clinic, or the market, or to church. She focused an unusual amount of preventive prayer on his condition. He thrived. And she enjoyed him immensely. Not once did any symptoms of an impending seizure occur. The time sped by rapidly, and soon the Clarks had brought to an end their joyous reunion with their older children, and had flown back to Nigeria. One can only try to imagine their feelings as they went to Mary's house to reclaim their child. Would he have been terribly homesick? Did Mary have major nursing problems which may have inconvenienced her? Were they right in imposing such a big responsibility on such a busy woman? Anticipation of seeing their son again and second thoughts about having left him caused some degree of consternation.

Upon arrival at Mary's, it was hard to believe their eyes. Their son looked healthy and happy, and spouted some words with a rather distinct American twang to them. They poured out their thanks to a gleaming Mary.

Mr. Clark, a fine gentleman, took out his wallet and attempted to pay Mary for her invaluable services which they knew could not be bought with money. Mary politely, but firmly, refused any payment, saying that she did not entertain their son for the sake of remuneration. He countered, saying, "If you will not accept money, can you think of something I can do for you to express our gratitude?" That was a question framed in Heaven! Mary was ready with an answer.

"Yes." she said, "I believe you have the authority to do something that I need very urgently."

"What is that, Mary?"

"You have lots of connections with important people in the Education Department of the government, and I do not. I would like to gain official permission to teach the Bible in three government schools in this area—Tilden Fulani, Ribina, and Jarawin Kogi. I would like to teach at the same hours when the Muslim teachers are having Koranic classes with the Muslim children. As of now, the Christian children are just released to the playground at those periods, and I could be teaching them God's Word," Mary explained with enthusiasm.

Mr. Clark smiled widely and said, "Tomorrow I will go to Bauchi, the provincial capital, and see the head education officer, and I will report back to you tomorrow night! That sounds like a great idea!"

True to his word, he made the trip the next day, and returned in the evening with his face aglow, and his hands extending a precious document. A very clear statement met Mary's eyes, giving her assurance of authority to teach the Bible in the release-time classes at any school in Bauchi Province. She could only easily cope with the three schools she had mentioned, but she was happy for the blanket permission. It didn't take long before she set to work, preparing Child Evangelism lessons in the Hausa language, which she had learned after leaving K'woi. Jaba was not spoken in the Rinji area.

The classes began with a very good response from the children. Even some of the Muslim children came to hear the Bible stories. Mary was greatly encouraged until one day when she appeared at school and found her classroom empty. No students in sight. A Muslim teacher appeared to break the news to her that the children no longer wanted to attend her classes. She knew that that was a fabricated falsehood. She simply replied saying, "Alright, I will write to the chief education officer in Bauchi about this matter, as he gave me permission for this work." The Muslim teacher said he, too, would write. She mailed her letter promptly and waited for developments. Day after day the mail brought no reply.

Two long weeks elapsed. Then one afternoon a beautiful limousine pulled up in front of her house, and a man rushed up to Mary to say, "I've come to see you about this terrible thing that has happened."

"What terrible thing?" she asked.

"Your being hindered from teaching the Bible in the schools! Come, get into my car and we will go to see that teacher who told you that the classes had been stopped."

Mary obliged, settling into the spacious back seat of the car, surrounded by many soft cushions. "How did I suddenly deserve such luxury?" she wondered. They entered the school, and summoned the Islamic teacher. Seeing the beautiful sleek car with the official emblem, and the uniform of the official, the teacher bowed and scraped the ground in front of him, raising his arms up and down, saying, "Giwa! Giwa!" (meaning "elephant," a term used as a greeting to an important official). The unexpected visitor burst forth with his bombastic oratory, venting his authority in no uncertain words or volume. "Who do you think you are? This white lady received permission from the Bauchi Education Officer, the Bauchi District Officer, the Bauchi Resident Officer of Her Majesty the Queen's government, and from the Queen of England herself to teach the Bible!" (The inclusion of the Queen's name, Mary was sure, was not only hyperbole, but official big-mouthing). He continued, "Who gave you permission to rescind their order? You cannot hinder her from teaching!" More bowing and scraping and pronouncements of "giwa!" followed, and then the official said to Mary, "Come, I will take you home and you may resume your work tomorrow! You have been teaching three times weekly, but you may teach daily from now on!"

When Mary appeared at class the next day, the room was full of happily reinstated children. She couldn't have asked for better attentiveness. The results of that opening to teach at Rinji had widespread repercussions. Mary's permission to teach the Bible in government schools opened the door for reaching untold thousands of students in schools all over Nigeria. Christian Bible classes were held everywhere that teachers could be found to teach them during the release-time classes. Bible became a part of the scheduled curriculum for all students professing to be Christians, but many animists and Muslims also joined the classes. A little is a lot when God is in it! Mary added "Pioneer" to her many titles, and students will be forever grateful. Many of them are carrying on her work in classrooms as qualified Bible Knowledge teachers. Can success be measured by any better standard?

In her retirement, Mary has had visits from two Nigerians whose lives were profoundly impacted by her when they were young lads. Seeing them again and hearing of their steadfastness in the Faith, she felt like the Apostle John when he wrote, "I have no greater joy than to hear that my children are walking in the truth"-3 John,v.4. Years ago, while Mary was stationed at Rinjin Gani, she drove eight miles each week to a mining camp owned by Mr. Bill Barlow in order to teach the miners' children. One boy, "Son of Sunday," *('Dan Ladi* in Hausa, so named because he was born on a Sunday), was an especially bright boy. His father, Garba, was one of Mr. Barlow's employees. 'Dan Ladi literally seemed to gobble down everything he was taught. Mary readily saw great potential in him. She invited him to go with her to Rinjin Gani to attend school. His eyes like saucers and his smile as wide as his face, he quickly ran to get permission from his father for this unexpected privilege. Before long he was boarding at the home of Mary's cook, Gabar, 'Dan Filasu, galloping through grades 1 through 4 of the Primary School, and four years of Secondary School as well. Witnessing Mary's clinic work at Rinji, 'Dan Ladi entertained the hope of becoming a nurse. Mary arranged for his entrance at the Nurses' Training School at Vom, run by the Sudan United Mission. Most of the students at that time were male. Mary underwrote his expenses. His potential was evident to all the hospital staff. When he completed the Vom course, they sent him to England for advanced training. Sending nationals overseas for training can sometimes result in "brain drain," since they decide to stay where they are rather than to enrich their homeland, sharing the results of their studies. Not so with 'Dan Ladi. He returned to Vom. By that time the Government had taken over the mission hospital. His good record was taken into consideration, and he was installed as Administrator of the hospital. Later on, the Government returned the hospital to the S.U.M., but didn't release 'Dan Ladi. He was promoted to be the Minister of Health for Plateau State where he served faithfully for some years until political conditions changed and he was retired, replaced by a Muslim. That did not deter him from seeking God's next clear assignments for him. He was elected an elder of the Vom Church, a member of the Board of Governors of the Vom Christian Hospital, Chairman of the Board of Governors of the Mangu Leprosy and Rehabilitation Center at the Dr. Barnden Memorial Clinic of Jos, and teacher of English at an Extension Bible School in Jos. He and his wife are just now (1997) completing a six-year course of Bible Study at that same Extension School. He recently wrote Mary, saying, "Please pray for me, and thank God for choosing to use me even though I am retired. May His name be glorified, and He alone be exalted!"

Istifanus, 'Dan Bauchi, was the bright young son of Mary's clinic dispenser. He was a diligent student, learning quickly. Upon completing Secondary School at Rinjin Gani, he enlisted in the Nigerian Air Force. He worked himself up to a high teaching position. Mary recalls how, when he was a small child, she had taught him the rudiments of arithmetic. She drilled him on the number of pennies in a shilling and of shillings in a pound. But imagine, if you can, how she laughed with him when they reminisced together during his visit to her Sebring home! He had been sent to the USA by the Nigerian Air Force to purchase millions of dollars' worth of planes in California! She felt like apologizing for not having gone into the millions when she prepared counting examples for the apt young student so many years ago! Istifanus (meaning Stephen) remains an active Christian. Within the contingency of Nigerian pilots who came with him to California to purchase planes and then fly them back to Nigeria, he was the only Christian. He bore a good witness for his Lord to the other pilots. The Lord needs his lights in the sky as well as in the hospitals and the pulpits!

Who wouldn't be a missionary, leaving behind him a legacy of lives dedicated to God and to the blessing of their compatriots?

Mary's adobe brick house with corrugated iron roof at Rinjin Gani in Bauchi State, Nigeria.

Gabar, Mary's efficient cook, freed her to spend valued time in ministry. He is seen here with his family.

Mary held clinics regularly for 600 leprosy patients at Tilden Fulani, an outstation of Rinji. On this day a friend from New Zealand was helping to dispense the medicine while Mary kept the records. (1964)

13

Mary and the Leopard on the Dark Porch

Mary Haas spent most of her 43 years of missionary service at just two stations, 23 at K'woi and 20 at Rinjin Gani. We often nicknamed our Mission "Sure, I'll Move." Most workers did have to move more often than Mary did. But it fell to her lot one year to fill in for some furloughing missionaries for a period of seven months at Billiri, a northeastern center where SIM had Bible, Teacher Training, Elementary, and Secondary Schools, besides a hospital.

There was quite a photogenic hill at Billiri, a favorite target of visitors' cameras. At about 4:00 p.m. almost everyday, Mary noticed that a full-grown leopard enjoyed standing at its summit to survey the scene below. At night the leopard would descend to stalk whatever it could find to keep itself well fed. It would steal the villagers' goats and dogs. One night it stole the SIM nurse's pet dog. The Billiri townsmen were aware of the leopard's intentions, and tried with spears and arrows to fell it, but unsuccessfully. It always escaped to its secret lair.

One morning, while Mary was enjoying her early devotions, she heard a terrific thump. She went to the door and saw the leopard rounding the corner of the house, its jaws clamped tightly on the neck of Mary's pet cat. The cat always slept on a little table at the back of the house. An easy victim to grab!

Mr. Jack Nicholson from Gelengu, a neighboring station, was sleeping in a small ante-room at the time. He was an experienced hunter. Mary knew that he had a gun equipped with bullets big enough to kill a marauding elephant. "How providential that he is here," she thought to herself. She aroused him from a heavy sleep, saying, "Come with your gun! There's a leopard outside!". He came out of his room, drowsily shouting, "Where is it? Where is it?" The gun accidentally exploded, drilling a big hole in the cement floor only three or four inches from Mary's foot. Cement and rug fragments went flying through the room, and Mary tried to show him how close she had been to an amputation. "Never mind the floor or the foot!" he shouted, "I have another bullet!"

Mary and Jack both ran outside. (Not too smart a move!) The leopard tracks on the ground around the house revealed that the animal had retreated into the tall grass. They decided that it was much too dangerous to pursue him into the grass at that time.

One night, shortly after the incident, the staff set out to go to Kaltungo, about eight miles distant. Mr. Leslie Maxwell, Principal of Prairie Bible Institute of Three Hills, Canada was with them, as he had been invited to be their District Conference speaker. Mr. Maxwell was enjoying his African trip and decided to try his expertise at using a gun. He shot a crown bird which was stored in the car trunk and then hung up on the enclosed back porch at Billiri, with the intention that he would dress it the next day.

Shortly after Mary got into bed, she heard a distinct scratching sound. She arose, surveyed the porch, but the darkness revealed nothing. Back to bed she went, only to be aroused again in a short while by repeated scratching. Bravely but foolishly, she took a flashlight and went out onto the porch, only to be confronted, face to face, with the leopard, standing on its hind legs, and determinedly ripping the screen door to shreds. She screamed with all her might. A leopard isn't easily frightened, but this one had heard enough. He dashed away into the darkness.

Mr. and Mrs. Richins were visiting Billiri from a distant northern station, and sleeping in the guest room, about 50 yards from the porch. Mary trumpeted a desperate call for help. Bernice Thompson, a teacher, and Ida Trapp, the station nurse, came running from other parts of the station compound, followed by the Gerald Troutmans who had quickly robed themselves in raincoats and helmets. When all the gathering ones heard what the screams were about, they did not congratulate themselves for braving the darkness with a leopard nearby. But they gathered courage to go to the guest room to awaken Mr. Richins, since they knew he had a gun. They tied the dead crown bird to a tree so that the leopard would not do further damage to the porch. Mr. Richins joined all the other night owls in the sitting room where they sat, as quiet as mice, awaiting the return of the leopard. But, to their dismay, he did not accept their invitation to be shot. Evidently

Mary's screams, calling for help, had assuaged his hunger for crown bird meat that night.

That was not the last episode with that leopard. But about a month later, Mr. Jim Hilker, another experienced hunter from a neighboring station, Tula Wange, was driving along a road in that area when his car lights focused on the spotted leopard. One shot was all it took to rid Billiri of its predator of goats, dogs, and cats. In a zoo the staff could have appreciated the leopard's beauty, but meeting it on a dark porch while it was hungrily trying to steal a bird—that's a story only for dedicated conservationists.

No longer a threat, the leopard is stretched out for all to see.

14

Hawwa, the Little Fulani Girl

The Fulani cattle-herders of West Africa are a nomadic tribe. Their wealth is in their cattle. They move from place to place seeking pastureland. It is not as hard for them to move as it would be for Americans. They simply roll up their cornstalk house, and tie it on a cow's back. Another cow carries all their cooking utensils. The young children get a free ride on the cows' backs.

Hawwa was a little Fulani girl who moved around in that way. One day her people noticed that she had a spot on her face. Her father put salt on that spot, and pulled a cow up close to her face so that the animal could lick the spot until it became an open sore. The cow licked and licked, and the open sore appeared. It hurt a lot! But when it healed up, the spot still remained. The family finally realized that Hawwa had leprosy! They stuck a number of corn-stalks into the sandy soil to make a house where she would live, all by herself. They made a cornstalk fence around the house. They brought food to the lonely little girl every day, but she felt like a prisoner in her little drafty enclosure.

One day she heard two men's voices through the spaces between the corn stalks. They were talking about a big white house where white people lived, who could heal leprosy! They said the house was near Bauchi. She knew in which direction the city of Bauchi was, but she had never been there. She decided that she must go there. But she did not dare to tell any one.

Daily Hawwa put aside some of her mush, so that she would have something to eat on her way to Bauchi. She waited until a moonlight night, and she left when all the other members of her family were asleep. If they had seen her leaving, they would have stopped her. She hid in the tall grass during the daylight hours, and traveled only at night. She heard the hyenas' mournful cries. She knew that there were snakes crawling about, and all sorts of other night creatures. But, determined to reach her goal, she kept plodding on.

One morning she saw the big white house! It was the S.I.M. Bauch Leprosy Hospital. But fear filled her little heart, and she could not budge. From a distance she could see the white people moving about, helping sick folks. In the Lord's providence, a Christian woman from Miss Haas' station, Rinjin Gani (80 miles away), was at that Hospital, receiving treatment for leprosy. Her name was Pendu. Pendu was gathering a few sticks together for cooking her morning gruel when she spied Hawwa hiding among the tall grasses. She went close to the child who was shaking with fright. Gently she asked her why she was there. Hawwa told Pendu her story, but said she was too scared to go to the big white house.

Pendu calmed her fears and invited the child to stay in her hut with her. She related how the missionaries were helping many folks who were suffering from the same illness. Hawwa hesitated, but followed Pendu. The white strangers received her lovingly, and began daily treatments. Pendu's love for Hawwa was very tender, and it was not hard for Hawwa to love her in return. Pendu told her the amazing story of Jesus. Hawwa had never heard anything so wonderful before. Soon she accepted Jesus into her heart, and Pendu taught her how to read the Bible so that she could learn more about the Savior who had died for her, and was now alive with God in Heaven, and would soon return to this earth.

Hawwa heard the Christians joyfully singing the precious hymns, and she longed to own a hymnbook of her own. Pendu promised that she would give Hawwa a hymnbook if she memorized the Bible verses which she was teaching her. In a very short time she had earned her hymnal!

The day for Pendu's discharge arrived. She was free of leprosy! She returned to Rinjin Gani, leaving Hawwa at Bauchi to continue receiving her treatments. Later on, Hawwa's day of release came, and she longed to go to visit Pendu. She started out on her 80-mile trek alone, but this time she walked in the daylight hours, with the Light of the World in her heart. She reached Rinjin Gani, tired but happy. Pendu introduced her to Miss Haas, and they had joyous times of fellowship together. After a week's stay, Hawwa said that she would venture forth to look for her parents. She knew that they, like all nomadic

Fulanis, had moved on, but she had no idea where they were. Pendu prepared lots of food for her trip.

Hawwa had heard rumors about the direction in which her family may have traveled. She assured Pendu that she would inquire at every Fulani encampment as to their location. As she left, prayers followed her, but, sadly. no word was ever heard as to whether or not she had located her family. There was no mail service which she would have known how to use in order to make them aware of her whereabouts. The Fulani people were very resistant to the Gospel at that time, and there were no resident missionaries working specifically among them. Pendu and Miss Haas were left to rejoice in the knowledge that Hawwa's Savior would care for her. They expect to see her in Heaven someday.

The Fulani people are scattered widely throughout West Africa, presenting a big challenge to the Christian church. There are many "Hawwa"s among them. Most of the Fulanis are Muslims, very much in need of the Savior's love, and the prayers of all who know Him.

above: The duplex shared by Kay Herring and Mary Haas at the SIM retirement village, Sebring, Florida.

left: Mary's very dear friend, Kay Herring.

below left: Dan and Elizabeth Beall, Fort Myers, Fl., faithful prayer helpers and supporters through many years.

below right: Mary as she looked when she left Nigeria in 1968.

15

Retired and Retreaded

Mid-summer, 1968 found Mary with a second bout of eye trouble. She had undergone cataract surgery at the famous S.I.M. Kano Eye Hospital in northern Nigeria under the expert care of Dr. Benjamin Keitzman, the resident Opthalmologist. She needed to have her other eye cared for as well, but the Keitzmans had gone home to the U.S.A. She had already served the Lord in Nigeria from the age of 24, and was now 66 years old, a wee bit beyond the stipulated age for retirement. The Mission told her she could stay on longer, if she wished. She was very happy in the work at Rinjin Gani, just as she had been at K'woi. But as she pondered the issue and prayed, she thought that while she was still healthy and strong, she would like to get involved in some home ministries. Also, she would like to have Dr. Keitzman perform the second eye surgery.

Kay Herring was one of Mary's very close friends, and, incidentally, a very dear friend of the Jacobsons as well. They had worked with Kay for 15 years at Kagoro, which was about 35 miles from Mary's station, K'woi. When Kay had had serious eye trouble some time previous to Mary's similar case, Mary had accompanied her to Kano where she consulted the specialists there. At that time Mary promised Kay that if her eye problem worsened greatly, Mary would go wherever she was and take care of her. While Mary was deciding to leave Nigeria, Kay retired to the United States. Kay had inherited a legacy, given for the purpose of building a small duplex at the SIM Retirement Center in Sebring, Florida. She used the gift for that purpose, moved into one side of the duplex, and reserved the other side for her friend, Mary Haas.

Mr. and Mrs. Dan Beall from Ft. Myers learned from Mary of her plans to retire at Sebring, so they drove over out of curiosity to see what her new home would look like. They were well-impressed with the lovely village. But they noticed that Kay's "Florida room" had been enclosed, whereas Mary's was open, without walls, windows, or screens. So they telephoned Mary who was visiting her family in Ohio to find out if she would like her Florida room enclosed like Kay's. If so, they wanted to make it possible. "Yes, please!" was the answer. Another gracious, unsolicited provision from the Lord!

Mary pulled into the Sebring Retirement Center on Thanksgiving Day, one month after Kay had occupied her apartment, and one day after the work on her own apartment was completed. Mary was accompanied by her brother, Milford, who wanted to help her settle in. As they entered, no one was in sight, but it was easy to find Mary's house, since Milford's truck was parked outside. Milford had sent some of his employees ahead in his truck which was laden with the lovely new furniture he had provided from his store. The employees were found in the Fellowship Hall, along with all the village residents, enjoying a grand Thanksgiving dinner. Mary and Milford were invited to join the feast. What a warm welcome they received!

After dinner Milford's employees laid the carpet in Mary's apartment, and moved in all of her furniture. By evening Mary was well settled, and able to sleep in her own four-poster bed which she had received from the "Queen for a Day" TV program some years before. It had followed her home from Africa.

The SIM village had been open for only two years before Mary arrived. It was Dr. Raymond Davis who had the vision and burden for the project. He asked Dr. and Mrs. R V. Herbold to search for a suitable property, After an extensive search in several states, Sebring was chosen and Herbolds became the first Managers. Mrs. Herbold is still a resident. The other residents when Mary joined them were: Hazel Bell, Hazel Ryckman, Mrs. John Hay, Mr. and Mrs. Harold Ogilvie, Kay Herring, and Josephine Bulifant. The Richard Brandts arrived that same Fall to assume the Managership, as the Herbolds were retiring. The Harry Harlings, the Gordon Beachams, Sr., and the Harold Dancys all arrived that Fall as well. The only survivors of that list are Mary Haas and Gladys Herbold. Many residents have come since then, and passed into Glory. At this writing in February, 1997, the residents number about 150 here in Sebring. In the Carlsbad, California village there are about 30 retirees.

Mary settled very happily into the village life, enjoying her small, brand new apartment. Among her many nicknames is, "The Hostess with the mostest." That tiny kitchen fed scores of visitors and fellow residents. Fellowship with coworkers was very pleasant, indeed.

It wasn't long before Mary became a bit restless to become engaged in some specific ministry for the Lord. She saw an ad in the local paper, saying that the new Highlands Regional Medical Center needed volunteer helpers. She applied, paid her entry fee, was accepted, purchased her pink jacket and was formally declared a "Pink Lady," beginning her work immediately. She was on duty once or twice weekly, and kept that schedule faithfully for 22 years. Not bad for retreads!

As stated elsewhere, Mary has been a baseball fan since childhood, so many of her evenings were spent watching games on TV during baseball season. Whenever a group went to see a live game, she was along, shouting. The love of baseball became a very fine contact point with many of the male patients. They were amazed to hear Mary chatting with them about teams, players, and specific, outstanding plays. During the football season she found herself a bit less responsive, because she didn't really enjoy watching the roughness of football. However, while she held that job, she made it a point to be "up" on football news before going to work, and many a patient was glad to have some one to talk with about his favorite game. She could also hold her own fairly well in conversing about basketball or tennis. Nowadays she doesn't miss many ice skating competitions. She not only loves spectator sports, but she is a good sport in all the give and take of friendly conversation and interaction.

Kay and Mary went together to the office of Child Evangelism Fellowship, and asked for a class of black children. They conducted that class for ten years at the Methodist Church of DeSoto City, a section of Sebring, about seven miles from the SIM village. When they started, only two children appeared, but little by little the attendance grew to 40 enrollees. George and Mae Beacham joined them, assisting greatly. They all did visitation in the homes, getting to know the parents of the children, and were well-received.

Harry Elyea was living in Avon Park and had a big truck. At Halloween he went to the Methodist Church in the DeSoto section and filled the truck with Mary's Child Evangelism kids. They had a wonderful time "trick-or-treating" throughout the S.I.M. village. Another time George and Mae Beacham and Harry Elyea took the Child Evangelism class kids to Hammock Park in Sebring where the trees, foliage, etc. have been preserved to prove what Florida was like when it was first discovered. (A hammock is a piece of land, peculiar to the South, where hardwood trees grow.) There is an extensive boardwalk where one may see the cypress swamps up close, and observe snakes and alligators from a safe position on the boardwalk. Alas, on that occasion one of the little boys fell down from the walkway into the water below, too close for comfort to a reposing alligator! George Beacham's long arms came to the rescue. He is tall and lean. He reached down and plucked the dripping-wet child from the water and the potentially-grave danger. He was an instant hero!

Mary wasn't content with just two volunteer activities. When the Sebring Care Center opened (now known as Integrated Health Services) she was one of the first volunteers. Once a week for about ten years she faithfully discharged her duties, spreading cheer and helping in rehabilitating discouraged patients. Alta Dronen from the SIM village joined her. Together they often prepared food at home and took a carload of patients, with the permission of the authorities, to a picnic by the lake—a welcome change of scenery and association.

Mary's eyes kept roving, looking for more opportunities for service. She was attracted to the "Meals on Wheels" program. The Palms Retirement Home prepared the meals. Kay Herring, Ruth Veenker, Margaret Lange, and Mary delivered them by car to the disabled and shut-ins quite widely scattered throughout the Sebring area.

"New Hope" is another agency ministering to the elderly or infirm. For a period of time Mary joined their program of taking people shopping, to the bank, to medical appointments, etc.

When Mary first moved south she began attending the First Presbyterian Church of Sebring. She taught a Sunday School class of children, helped with Daily Vacation Bible School, and had turns holding offices in the Ladies' Missionary Society. Many people from that church hold her in high esteem. When she meets one of them in a store there is always a very friendly encounter, even though for the last five years she has attended the Covenant Presbyterian Church where she is an associate member. Once a month Mary and Gladys Herbold go out with several of the First Presbyterian Church women to enjoy a restaurant lunch together and to reminisce about by-gone days.

In January, 1997 Mary was asked to speak to the Covenant WiC, Women in the Church, who met in a home. By special request she told one of her stories from Africa. When she finished she was overwhelmed by the first standing ovation she ever recalls having received. Many voiced their request that her stories be put into a book.

As part of the Covenant Presbyterian Church outreach program, Mary has participated for several years in the "Angel Tree Project" at Christmas time. A tree bears cards with names and ages of the children of local prisoners, plus the name of an item of clothing or a toy which a child would love to have. Mary takes one of those cards and does her shopping with great joy, wraps her gift and either delivers it to the home personally, or takes it to the church to be delivered with other gifts.

For the last two years she has also gotten a great deal of pleasure from taking part in the "Samaritan's Purse" project, "Operation Christmas Child." This year one million shoe boxes containing toys, books, crayons, clothing, toothpaste and brush, or whatever the buyer wishes to give, were distributed in Bosnia, Russia, and many other lands where war or poverty have robbed children of the joys known to American children. Samaritan's Purse works all year long in needy lands all over the globe, digging wells, building medical clinics, supplying medical personnel for various projects, taking food and medicine wherever disaster has struck, etc. Franklin Graham, Billy Graham's son, is the President.

The first several years Mary was at Sebring she helped Mr. Brandt by going regularly to the Orlando or Tampa Airport to meet incoming visitors or new residents, or to take people to departing flights. She was never happier than when she was behind the wheel of her car, especially if she had the opportunity to minister to some one's need.

In 1993, at age 92. Mary decided on her own to sell her car and give up driving, even though her license was still valid for four more years. She said, "I'd rather stop myself than to be told to stop driving!" She purchased a three-wheel electric scooter for easy maneuvering within the confines of the SIM village. She has plenty of friends, willing and able to take her where she needs to go outside of the village.

Retirement sometimes leads to early demise when the abrupt change of schedule and relinquishing of responsibility makes one feel unneeded. It's easy to see that Mary avoided those dire aspects of retirement by constant spiritual renewal and by making herself available for service in previously untried projects.

"Always give yourselves fully to the work of the Lord, because
you know that your labor in the Lord is not in vain"
—1 Cor. 15:58.

The present residents carry on the tradition of keeping busy. Almost every one is involved in church membership, and various ministries within the church. Quite a few hold jail services in one or more of Florida's 80 Correctional facilities, either for men or for women. One works in the Administrative office once a week. Two men minister to the prisoners during their work detail assignments. Another missionary works five days a week in the Education Department of a large facility.

Several of our residents have one-on-one sessions with migrants, teaching English as a second language. A few of us are writing memoirs, either our own or some one else's. Several are engaged in Translation work, preparing an Old Testament Commentary in the Hausa language for use in West Africa. At least four of our retired nurses still take their turns helping the nursing staff regularly with the care of the residents, giving shots and other treatments, taking patients to see their doctors, helping with record keeping, etc.

Our Lodge is under the capable direction of Don and Jean TerMeer. Many women use their "Gifts of help" in the Lodge, ministering to those not able to care for certain needs totally, or helping in the kitchen or laundry. Several women lift the morale of the weak ones by giving them haircuts and perms, etc, or cutting their nails. Some of the residents have golf carts for getting around in the village. They use them often in distributing mail from the office. Several spend valued time reading to those whose eyesight has failed. Several man the "Hot-line," relaying urgent messages regarding sickness or death.

The village Nursing Staff is comprised of four nurses who keep their credentials up-to-date. They are, through the Head Nurse, Elaine Douglas, in ready touch with the mission doctor at the Charlotte, NC headquarters. The 60 or 70 local doctors consulted by the patients throughout the year often remark about the excellent record-keeping by the nurses. If some one has to go to the Emergency Room, or into the hospital, his record of illnesses and current medications goes with him, making his care much more simple and efficient.

A lovely tradition has developed at Christmas time. About two weeks before Christmas, a date is set for all the ladies to bring a plateful of cookies to the Fellowship Hall. Large platters are set out on the long dining tables. The ladies encircle those tables over and over again, distributing the scores of platefuls of mostly homemade cookies, candy and nuts to the platters. When all have been used up, the wrapping with plastic begins, and a number of drivers are assigned by the nurses to deliver the platters, along with a Christmas greeting and an appropriate leaflet. It is not unusual to hear the doctors or their staff say, "We've been waiting for you!" For the next few prayer meeting nights, notes of thanks from the doctors will be read to the residents by the Manager.

One of the former staff nurses gives foot care every few weeks. Several of the men make themselves available to keep the cars clean, or to do repairs on electric appliances. Many are on the nurses' lists for driving those who have no cars to their doctors' appointments. A lot of folks take turns on the "Neighborhood Watch" during church services or prayer meetings. One lady cares for the book orders at the three Bible Conferences held each year. A gentleman always gives his services for leading the singing at those conferences, while several gifted musicians play the piano and organ. Another gentleman records all the messages given during those special times of blessing, and makes copies of the tapes, as requested. Others serve as ushers. We don't have custodians for the chapel or the Fellowship Hall, so the residents respond when a cleaning day is announced. Nor do we have guards at our entrances, but the gates which need locking in the evening are cared for by residents. All of these jobs are good for the compound, and good therapy for those who want to avoid rusting away from inactivity. When we have a compound dinner, a menu is drawn up and all the women sign up for the item they will bring. Many hands make light work! The more we are involved in the daily life of the village, the better we feel!

A Social Committee exists to plan outings or times of relaxation, or celebrations of special milestones. Every other week we view a Video, the subjects ranging from the sublime to the almost-ridiculous (to keep us laughing!) Our nurses endorse the Scriptural concept that laughter is good medicine!

Our village has been called, "The Prayer Capital of the World." Hyperbole or not, it is a place where individuals exercise the greatest privilege known to man—that of entering God's presence and proceeding to his majestic Throne without fear or special favor. Groups gather also to pray specifically for various needs. There's a Muslim World Prayer time; a Francophone prayer meeting (for the lands where French culture and language are emphasized); one for the work of SIM in Latin America; one for Ethiopia and the Sudan; another for Asia; yet another for the children and grandchildren of residents; one for translation work. The regular Thursday evening prayer meeting, under the direction of our beloved Manager, Garth Winsor, is attended by all residents and their visitors. At this latter meeting, David John, our prayer leader, lines up all of the circular letters from all over the SIM world. As folks come into the Chapel, they can take one of the letters and pray orally or in private for the needs. A news sheet, prepared by the Manager's very efficient wife, covers village needs, plus a page of current prayer requests from the SIM Headquarters in Charlotte, North Carolina. That is passed out to every one in an effort to keep us all abreast of personal or mission-wide needs. Attending that prayer meeting is a blessing in itself.

Lest I give the impression that we are in a holier-than-yours location of perfection, let me mix my thankfulness for this wonderful environment with the reality we all recognize—we are sinners saved by the unmerited grace of the loving God. He has favored us to be His witnesses. Along the way, as many years have unfolded, His grace and mercy have been absorbed in measure (there's a lot more to be absorbed!). We rejoice if some of the fruitfulness of knowing and serving Him is evident to others. The praise and glory are His! God calls Himself "the God of all the earth." He wants to be the God of every individual. If even just one reader of this book has become aware that he or she does not enjoy a personal relationship with God through Jesus Christ, we want to invite that one to "Taste and see that the Lord is good; blessed (happy) is the man who takes refuge in him" — Psalm 34:8. If such should occur, the subject of this book, Mary Haas, and the writer would rejoice exceedingly!

One of the pleasant aspects of a closely knit community like ours is the very evident care for one another. At birthday time, one needs to clear off a place to display his cards, which invariably cheer and encourage. When some one loses a loved one, cards and help with meals are the order of the day. When some are hospitalized or in a nursing home, the number of visitors from the village going to check on them is a source of testimony to the love which glues us together. When a resident is promoted to Glory, a beautiful memorial service is held. The Manager prepares a précis of the departed one's life and service, and we all feel that we know that one even better than when he or she was with us. The residents' cars line up behind the hearse and follow police escorts to one of the two burial grounds in Sebring. A service follows at the grave as we experience sweet sorrow. It is sweet because it is not a final "Goodbye," but rather a committal until we meet again in Christ's presence.

"All men will know that you are my disciples if you love one another"—John 13:35.

To all who have worked to make this Retirement Village possible, abundant thanks are due. Countless volunteers have come to share their expertise, their time and their labors in building projects, road-construction, plumbing and electrical installation, repairs of all kinds, window-washing, helping the infirm, etc. Only the Lord knows the extent of dedication involved. Donors have given priority to the re-sponsibility of being good stewards, making our labors on the mis-sion field as well as our comfort and enjoyment of retirement pos-sible. Their left hands may not know what their right hands have given, but the Lord knows and will reward them accordingly. In the mean-time, we will enjoy their efforts with unmitigated gratitude.

We would be remiss if we failed to acknowledge the valuable help and good service of the four steady employees who keep our village looking presentable and pleasant. The Manager and his wife, the Host-ess, are missionaries who served the Lord in Niger and in Nigeria under SIM. They agreed to a Home Assignment here at Sebring. They are grateful for the good team of workers who never fail to provide reli-able services. Jerry, Dan, Susan, and Beverly are not members of SIM, but have won the right to become beloved members of our Village family, greatly appreciated. Their jovial attitudes cheer us daily. Thank you, Lord!

"The hostess with the mostest" entertains often. Bill and Dottie Lockard are seen here at Mary's.

Below: Mary with TEAM missionary, Mrs. Conrad, by the "Angel Tree" at Covenant Presbyterian Church, Sebring, Florida.

Mary is always "game" for a game. Here she pits her vigor against Beverly Brandt's.

Fourty-eight trays of Christmas goodies, ready to be delivered to doctors' offices in thanks for their services. Sixty-five trays were delivered in 1997.

Above: The village Chapel where three Bible Conferences are held annually, attracting many Sebring friends. The Chapel was built by the Christian Businessmen's Association so that the Community could share the blessings of the excellent Bible teaching at the Conferences, conducted by SIM, Sebring. Our weekly village prayer meeting is held there, but no church has been established in the village. The residents participate in many different area churches.

Left: Norma Jones, village resident, and fellow Pandorian, frequently stops in to share the Ohio newspapers with Mary. They have many mutual acquaintances.

'Dan Ladi, whom Mary sponsored for medical training in Nigeria, later became medical supervisor for Plateau State. This was taken at Mary's house in Sebring when he visited her some years ago.

16

Seeing the U.S. At Last!

The slogan reminds us to "See the U.S.A. first!" Good idea. But usually young recruits for the mission field are rushing after completing their studies, trying to get out to their fields as soon as possible. No time to see the beauties of the U.S.A.! Some do very little traveling within their assigned country, since the work locally absorbs their time and energy completely. Both Mary and her side-kick, Kay Herring, determined upon their arrival in Florida, that while they had the health to do so, they would explore as much of the state as they possibly could. They rarely let the car tires cool off for long.

They were a good team. Kay came up with an assignment for the front passenger seat — "The one at the right reads the signs and pays the fines!" In spite of wearing out many sets of tires, no fines were ever levied. As said before, Mary was never happier than when she held the steering-wheel in her hands. Her car traveled in every direction. Not much of Florida missed their inspection. From east to west and north to south they enjoyed the public attractions, parks, the oceanside, and the fishing sites. They made many trips to Cypress Gardens, often taking visitors with them. They often traveled to St. Petersburg to visit Kay's brother.

Kay was a delightful travel companion, but she had no sense of direction. One day they set out to go to a store on Route 27 south. But when they got to R. 27, Kay insisted that they turn left (north). Mary humored her and kept driving until they almost reached the center of Avon Park, 11 miles from Sebring. Finally Kay admitted that she must have been mistaken, and a U-turn was made. They returned south, chuckling all the way.

Having covered Florida quite thoroughly, Mary and Kay set their sights on other states—Georgia, the Carolinas, Tennessee. Each trip was delightful. From 1968 when they arrived in Sebring until March 16, 1976, the two friends enjoyed one another fully. On that day, after attending an SIM Conference meeting, a film was shown which

Mary had already seen. She decided to go home, whereas Kay said she would stay for the film. Upon exiting the chapel, Kay discovered that it was raining quite steadily. She was portly, but able to move quickly, so she ran, trying to reach her house before getting thoroughly soaked. She arrived at her door, but collapsed. She tried to call Mary, but Mary, a very sound sleeper, didn't hear her calling. Kay managed to get inside to call Helen Vetter, the village nurse, who answered her phone and dashed over to Kay immediately. She suspected that Kay had had a heart attack, so she awakened Mary who went with her to take Kay to the Emergency Room of the Hospital. Kay was admitted, and Mary returned home to spend a suspense-filled night. The next day Mary went to visit Kay. The nurse asked if she was a close friend and Mary said, "Yes, we live together." The nurse said, "Good, maybe she will respond to your voice." Mary went in to Kay's room, but Kay was well on her way to the Father's house, and breathed her last earthly breath that afternoon, March 17th. For Kay it was "Far better!" For Mary it meant separation from her closest companion, and much adjustment.

Kay had always been a favorite in the S.I.M. To our family she was "Auntie Kay," and no one was more welcome in our Kagoro home. Her laugh rings in my ears as I write. Her eyes twinkled with mischief. One day when our youngest daughter, Nancy Kay, (named after Kay Herring) was about four years old, we went to Zonkwa, about 20 miles from Kagoro. Kay was in charge there at the time, and welcomed us with smiles and hugs. She noticed that both Jim and I were especially tired, having been unusually busy for some weeks. So she ordered us to the little guest room to rest, and said she would care for Nancy. Our three older daughters were away at school, and Nancy wasn't sure she wanted us out of her sight. Kay enticed her into her room where a big trunk stood, and said they would have a party. Nancy said it wasn't her birthday quite yet, but Kay said, "Well, we must have a celebration before we can have your birthday!" Kay unloaded the trunk with all kinds of things she could use for the occasion. Anne Sanders, her co-worker, made a cake, and soon the first of many "celebrations" which preceded birthdays in the Jacobson family had been inaugurated. Always with a special tribute in our hearts to our beloved "Auntie Kay Herring!"

The enlargement of the Fellowship Hall at the Sebring Retirement Village was dedicated to the memory of dear Kay Herring, and her picture hangs there, bringing back happy memories of a woman who left a very large mark on the history of the church in Nigeria, especially among the women whom she served as sponsor of the *Zumuntar Mata* (Women's Fellowship) which still thrives.

After Kay's promotion to Glory, her part of the Sebring duplex was used as a guest room, so Mary had close contact with many visitors. The love of travel continued in Mary's mind, and she found a willing passenger in Sadie Hay, the widow of John Hay. The John Hays were the parents of Ian Hay, the SIM General Director for many years, and presently General Director Emeritus.

At Fort Pierce a former SIM missionary, Miss Gillette, had a huge dog which required "animal-sitters" from time to time. Miss Gillette often made long trips to such places as Israel on research projects. She would call Mary to ask if she could care for the dog in her absence. Her lovely home was on the oceanside, so it wasn't hard for Mary to accept the invitation. Mrs. Hay was more than happy to go to Fort Pierce on the canine assignments. They always enjoyed one another immensely.

Five months after Kay Herring's death, Ruth Veenker arrived and was assigned to live in Kay's apartment. Ruth had been the first certified Elementary School teacher at K'woi. She and Mary had a great deal in common. She enjoyed travel, and so the car rolled away on many more trips, especially to Georgia where they were always welcomed warmly at Faith Valley. That wonderful place of spiritual refreshment had been founded by Alline Marshall and Bonnie Hanson. Many organizations gratefully enjoyed the beauty and hospitality there during retreats, and still do so.

Friendship is a marvelous gift from the Lord as two or more hearts are bonded together. When terminal illness threatens the connection, the parties involved suffer conflicting emotions. Ruth Veenker had been at Sebring for eight years when she became seriously ill in 1984. The diagnosis was leukemia, which progressed very rapidly. She was taken to Winterhaven Hospital. Ray, her dear brother, and Lois Veenker, his wife, also SIM Sebring residents, took Mary with them daily to visit her. In about two weeks the disease claimed Ruth's mortal body, leaving the three stunned. In December, 1984 the mission family gathered with the ambivalent feelings of joy because Ruth had gone to Glory, and sorrow because a great gap had been left in their lives. Mary and Ruth Veenker had traveled together many times, but Ruth was escorted to the Lord's presence by unseen messengers from God. Her pain and suffering vanished in a moment.

Ruth Webb was another travel companion. Mary traveled with her to North Carolina, along with Lucille Cain and Helen Vetter, sightseeing and enjoying the beauties of nature. Fortunately, Mary's memory is keen, enabling her to relive many of those happy excursions.

Every year Mary drove to Ohio to visit her brother, sometimes travelling with Mary Ellen Adams, and Burness Kampen. Mary was welcomed by relatives and friends in Ohio, and was kept busy visiting. She is, indeed, a favorite daughter of that part of Ohio.

Age did not erase Mary's wanderlust. In 1993 the SIM celebrated its 100th anniversary with a great gathering at the national Headquarters in Charlotte, NC. Mary was about to celebrate her 93rd birthday, but wouldn't consider missing that reunion of fellow workers. Being the oldest participant there, she was feted with the honor of cutting the immense anniversary cake at the main meeting. She also took part in a skit, depicting various phases of the ministry in Nigeria. Helen Vetter, Mary and I traveled to Charlotte for that epochal event. From there we went to Pandora, Ohio to visit Mary's brother, Milford, about whom I had heard so much. Fatigue wasn't allowed to hinder our following our ambitious plans to visit relatives in Virginia, and Georgia. After about two weeks we pulled into Sebring, overwhelmed with gratitude for the Lord's gracious protection.

Mary had visited Florida thoroughly in previous years, but in 1995 she repeatedly said that she would love to go to Key West again. My Oldsmobile Cutlass Ciera carried Irene Garrett, my dear friend from the Bradenton Missionary Village, Mary, and myself to Venice, Florida to see my brother and his wife, and then on to the Keys. It was Mary's third trip there. She found many changes and much increased commercialism. We were disappointed not to be able to see the famous coral seabeds on our boat trip because of rough waters.

That trip to the Florida Keys calmed Mary's intense desire to be on the move. She has been comparatively settled in her wee apartment since then, with only trips to baseball games, a rodeo and to the Christmas and Easter presentations at First Baptist Church of Orlando to break the daily routine. Instead of her going afar to visit friends, many of them come to her apartment. She is now filling her fourth guest book with names of her visitors. On Sunday afternoons Mary and I often rev up the "Olds" and go wherever the twist of the steering wheel takes us, along roads not familiar to us. So far we have managed to find our way home without the help of a rescue squad. Though Mary maintains that her travelling days are over, she is presently on a trip to Ohio! More power to you, Mary. Don't let your wings be clipped!

Mary had the honor of cutting the 100th Anniversary cake at SIM, Charlotte, NC Headquarters.

Mary with her beloved brother, Milford, in Pandora, Ohio, 1993.

17

Mary's Not Ruth-less

Lacking statistics to prove my point, I rely on conjecture that "Ruth" is an old-fashioned name, rarely affixed to a 1990s' baby. But it must have been extremely popular in the 1920s! I became Ruth #8 when I arrived at Sebring's SIM Retirement Village in 1989. Three other Ruths of this village have already passed on to Glory. In contrast, we have only two Marys in the village.

Mary Haas, coincidentally, was drawn to a number of Ruths who became close friends. The first one was Ruth Bixel who was a member of Mary's Ohio home church and Sunday School class. Their early bond was a cohesive one. They did not attend the same grade school, as Mary was in the Mt. Cory District school of Pandora, while Ruth was in the Pandora Elementary and High Schools. Ruth went on to obtain a doctorate in music and taught in many places, including the Grace Bible School of Omaha, Nebraska. Ruth always looked forward to Mary's furloughs from Nigeria for renewal of their friendship. It was during a visit to Mary's house in Sebring that Ruth became engaged to her own sister's widower, Raymond Miller. The match was a good one for both of them. Ruth's step-children and step-grandchildren totaled 19, all of whom celebrated her 90th birthday in gala style in December, 1996 in Sarasota where Ruth, now a widow, lives.

Ruth enjoyed travel as much as Mary did. One year she made arrangements through Menno Travel Service to meet Mary in Cairo on her way home for furlough. Mary first had an enjoyable stopover in Khartoum, Sudan in East Africa, visiting SIM missionaries before proceeding to Cairo. In Egypt she and Ruth did extensive sightseeing, in-

Ruth Bixel Miller usually spends her Dec. 25th birthday with Mary. This was her 89th. Photo: Norma Jones

cluding riding on "Rose," a camel which lacked the fragrance associated with roses! They entered every pyramid open to the public.

From Cairo they traveled to Jordan where Mrs. Erma Schneck Lambie was their gracious hostess. This trip took place shortly after the Six-Day War. Behind the Lambie house was an Arab Refugee Camp. Erma and her husband, Dr. Tom Lambie, were former SIM missionaries, later ministering in Palestine. Dr. Lambie was a renowned physician with a notable reputation as a public speaker and author. At the time of Mary and Ruth's visit, he was already in Glory. Erma made available to her guests the car which the Billy Graham team had given her. Her able chauffeur took the women to all the sites of Biblical interest, including places not usually seen by tourists.

At Qumran, the famous archeological site in the foothills northwest of the Dead Sea, the chauffeur told them the story of the little boy who had discovered the Dead Sea Scrolls in the long-neglected cave in which they were then standing. Qumran was originally an Iron Age Fort, dating back to the 6th century B.C. In the late second century B.C. it was occupied by a monastic community, known as the Essenes. In A.D. 68 the buildings were burned by the Romans. The monastic library had once contained the Dead Sea Scrolls, but they had been hidden for safekeeping in caves. They were not discovered until 1947. The driver related the story with the animation of personal involvement, to the astonishment of Mary and Ruth. He said that the little boy had taken the scrolls to his (the driver's) father. His father was illiterate and could not appreciate their potential value. However, with uncanny wisdom he directed the boy to take them to a museum. The rest is history! The scrolls were a news sensation to the entire world. They have been the object of close scholastic scrutiny, and a magnet for tourists. Their value in corroborating evidence of the accuracy of Scripture cannot be doubted. In recounting the story, the chauffeur mused wistfully about how wealthy his family could have been had they realized the scrolls' value and sold them to the museum. He took a picture of Mary and Ruth, sitting in the Qumran cave entrance, looking out at the Dead Sea in the distance.

Shortly after making my notes for this chapter I was in New York City, and had the opportunity to visit the American Bible Society Headquarters. A very large room there had been filled with mockups of the

Qumran hills, the caves. the shelves which had held the jars containing the hidden scrolls, etc. Translations of sections of the scrolls were on display.

In visiting Palestine, it had been necessary for Mary and Ruth to travel first to Jordan because it was illegal to enter Israel directly from Egypt. When they finished their sightseeing there, they went to the bridge which connected the two sections of the land. Their baggage was placed in the center of the bridge, to be picked up by Israelis on the other side. Then the women walked across the bridge into Israel. Many exciting tours to places they had known only through reading the Scripture became a vital part of their own personal experience.

In Jerusalem the two friends were sitting beside the Garden Tomb one day, reading the thrilling Resurrection story from God's Word. A tour group arrived. One of the tourists said to them, "Aren't you lucky to have your Bible along to read at this wonderful place!" The leader of the group overheard and asked Mary to read the Resurrection story aloud to the entire group. That sacred spot echoed again with the immortal words spoken by the angel, "He is not here, He is risen!" She continued the reading to include the encounter between her namesake, Mary Magdalene, and the Lord who directed her to "go and tell" the disciples that He had risen. What a thrill for Mary Haas to hear her own voice, reiterating that command whose words had sent her as His witness to Africa!

Secondly, we come to Ruth Veenker whom we have mentioned in another chapter. She was Mary's co-worker at K'woi in Nigeria. As stated, upon her retirement Ruth Veenker moved into the half of the duplex in Sebring which had belonged to Kay Herring. It was natural that Ruth would fit into the pattern of keeping active and mobile. Mary was happy to have a replacement in the car seat where the rider "reads the signs and pays the fines." They had many good times together, especially on the trips to Georgia and the Faith Valley. Ruth's sudden

Ruth Veenker became Mary's duplex partner after Kay passed away.
Photo: L. Veenker

illness with leukemia and her early departure to the Lord's presence left another empty spot in Mary's heart and activities.

In 1987 a four-plex (four apartments under one roof) was built at Sebring, attached to The Lodge where extra help was available to those who needed it. Mary was ready for a move to an apartment where less outdoor upkeep would be required. She had always maintained a beautiful garden, hedges, fruit trees, etc. She had the mistaken notion that the new apartments were only available to married couples. She chatted one day with the former General Director, Ray Davis, about the matter and he said, "Go for it!" But Mary jokingly replied, "I would have to be married long enough to make the move, and who would have me at age 86?" He contacted SIM Headquarters for verification of policy, and within a week of that conversation in November, 1988, Mary had contentedly settled into a lovely apartment, without the bother of planning a wedding to get there! Amazingly, she found that she had more kitchen space for her perpetual entertaining than she had had in the duplex.

Three months later, another Ruth (myself) arrived on a visit to Sebring for the purpose of deciding where to live following a proposed move to the village in August, '89. Manager Wally Braband, and Mike, the husband of my very close friend, Alice Glerum, persuaded me to consider one of the two empty apartments of the four-plex, since I was still convalescing from a heart attack. Added to their strong arguments was the persuasive protection of Mary Haas' "mother-hen wings." She begged me to move into Apartment "C" as her neighbor. The decision was finalized. It was a rather traumatic move, but the Lord graciously intervened in myriad details. I weathered the separation from family, and was soon welcomed by Mary to Sebring. From the start, Mary included me in all her entertaining and activities. We took turns, and still do, preparing our noon and evening meals

Mary with Ruth Jacobson in front of the fourplex. Mary's "green thumb" maintains the flowers.

which we share together. More than 18 years separate us age-wise, but we scarcely realize it, since Mary remains a dynamic gadabout. Some one told me upon my arrival, "Don't think that you can keep up with Mary Haas, because you can't!"

The almost eight years Mary and I have had together, as of this writing in 1997, have been filled with fellowship, ministry, and fun. Mary helped me to adjust to the absence of family around me, though I would dearly love to have that dimension of my life restored, too! I endeavor to make an annual visit to each daughter and her husband, enjoying all of my thirteen grandchildren.

Some people have an easily recognized "gift of helps." The fourth "Ruth", Ruth Grimshaw, is such a person. She started filling in for me during my occasional absences from Sebring, providing company for Mary and help in preparing meals. As time went on and Mary's strength waned a wee bit, Ruth did shopping for her and watered her flowers, etc. Mary often says, "I don't know what I'd do without her!" Ruth is a spreader of cheer everywhere she goes. She grew up in Africa as the daughter of Africa Inland Mission workers in the Congo. She later lived at the Westervelt home for missionary children in Batesburg, South Carolina and attended High School and Bible School there. She spent most of her years of SIM missionary service in Nigeria, teaching in a vernacular Bible School. At Sebring she circulates in her little golf cart all over the compound, doing errands, delivering mail, etc. In the process she has become a storehouse of local news. What we don't know about the village we hear from Ruth Grimshaw. The Lord has blessed us with so many precious friends, each contributing uniquely to our lives and our comfort.

The fifth Ruth was mentioned in another chapter in connection with a trip which Mary made with Ruth Webb. This Ruth hailed from Detroit, Michigan. She was not content to retire too comfortably. She had worked closely with Kay Herring, (Mary's former Sebring duplexmate) at Kagoro among the women, and later had served at the Jos Headquarters of SIM, Nigeria. Office work was in her blood. She found a wonderful opening for service at the Covenant Presbyterian Church (Presbyterian Church of America) in Sebring as secretary to the Pastor. She held that position admirably for eight or nine years. Once in a while Mary rides with Ruth to a church service or other function.

Aggregately, we who own the name, "Ruth," could hardly boast that we had reciprocated by providing Mary the same measure of blessing which she has given us. But at least we — Ruth Miller, Ruth Veenker, Ruth Grimshaw, Ruth Webb, and I, Ruth Jacobson — are glad that Mary didn't object to the monotony of being so often with a Ruth!

Ruth Jacobson, Ruth Webb, and Ruth Grimshaw

18

Fringe Benefits

The joys and blessings of being called by the Lord include being commissioned by His church, welcomed by a people soon to become one's own, and enabled by the Holy Spirit. More than enough to counterbalance any "sacrifices" or "deprivations" caused by leaving one's own family and homeland! Yet the Lord, "The giver of every good and perfect gift" delights in heaping extra, often unexpected blessings upon His servants. Mary Haas had many memorable travel experiences on her way to and from Africa. These were enriching, exciting, and enlightening. They became cause for praise to her Lord for His creation, His provision, and His constant protection.

Unless one were an international news reporter, an inveterate world traveller, or a corporate salesperson, it would be unusual to have visited 28 countries besides one's own. But Mary spent varied periods of time in Austria, the Azores, Belgium, Brazil (3 weeks), Canada (twice), Congo, the Canary Islands, Denmark, Egypt, England (3 times), France, Germany, Ghana, Italy, Jordan, Liberia, Morocco, Nassau in the Bahamas, the Netherlands, Nigeria, Norway, Palestine, Puerto Rico, Scotland (twice), Sierra Leone, the Sudan, Switzerland (3 times), and Yugoslavia. For none of these trips were mission funds utilized. Specially designated gifts from friends or family enabled Mary to see other parts of the world en route to or from her four-year terms of service in Africa.

Her first such venture was undertaken with Faye Moyer of the Church of the Brethren Mission. She was later to become the SIM Education Secretary in Nigeria. That trip covered the land of Mary's father's birth, Switzerland. He had been born at Berne, and Mary was thrilled to see the site of his birthplace. She visited quite a few hitherto-unknown relatives. She attempted to communicate in Swiss-German which she had learned as a child, but had not spoken for years. Her hearers graciously endured her mistakes with good humor. At times she found herself trying to talk to them in Jaba, the language she learned in Nigeria, but that did not bring a response!

Mary and Faye went next to Belgium where they visited a missionary from Pandora, Ohio, Mary's home town. Holland was their third stop, and Mary located quite a few of her father's relatives, who welcomed her warmly. She was keenly interested to find many "Haas Jewelry Stores." The trip ended with sightseeing in France and a take-off by plane to the USA and an always wonderful welcome by family and church friends.

A first trip with Ruth Bixel Miller to Egypt and Palestine was described in a previous chapter. The second such adventure, for which Ruth again made all the arrangements, featured two months' travel through Europe. They marvelled at the majestic beauty of Yugoslavia as they rode throughout the length of it by train. Ruth had obtained a "Eurail Pass" which enabled them to view Europe without the hassle and fatigue of driving. They found rail travel to be very pleasant. Rome and Venice, Italy were included in their itinerary. At the latter place they couldn't miss the graphic opportunity to ride in a gondola along a canal. Everywhere they went they were impressed with little parks, verdant with grass, breaking the monotony of bricks and mortar in the crowded urban areas. Flower beds interrupted the hurried stride of many pedestrians as they stopped to enjoy the flaming colors and neat patterns. Window boxes brightened most homes, adding color to otherwise mundane settings.

In France they rode by bus through the famous Arc de Triomphe. They saw the latest French styles and tasted French cuisine.

The beauty of the Scandinavian countries, Denmark, Sweden, and Norway, was memorable, especially the fjords. Their visit to Germany was highlighted by the six-hour presentation of the Lord's Passion at Oberammergau. They sat outdoors, unprotected from the cold, except by the blankets provided by their hotel. Less professional productions of the Passion have little appeal to those who have seen Oberammergau.

The big treat in London was attendance at a live performance of "The Sound of Music!" Delightful! In spite of that special exposure to the play, Mary can still enjoy the video or the occasional TV presentation of the film!

Mary and Ruth's sense of humor came into action as their train sped past the breath-taking beauty of Switzerland. Far more glorious than any camera could portray! Both of them could understand Swiss German fairly well, but, just for fun, they decided to feign ignorance of the language. When the conductor came into their compartment to check their Eurail Pass, he said to the several Swiss passengers sharing their compartment, "We have to watch these American tourists! They often cheat!" The two, wrongfully accused by association, remained innocently blank-faced. When they disembarked, Mary and Ruth bid farewell to the conductor in clear Swiss German. Guess what hues of brilliant color they noted on his face! They had to wait until they were out of reach of his ears to unstifle their pent-up laughter. It wasn't easy. Seeing the conductor so uncomfortable, they decided not to try that trick again.

Mary's next very-long-distance travel will probably take her to the portals of Heaven, her desired Haven. But, in the meantime, she is always ready to be "on the go!"

"When will we make that trip to Orlando to attend a service at First Presbyterian Church?"

"When can we go on a picnic to Vero Beach?" (where she has a cousin).

"Ruth Miller is always asking when we can visit her at Sarasota."

"You and I have still not gone to Georgia together to visit the MacDonalds at Douglas, nor the women at "Faith Ventures.""

"I hope we can go to Fort Myers soon to visit my cousins, Grace Haas and Katherine Edwards!"

Do these sound like the remarks and questions of a ninety-five-year-old who has outgrown her "Get up and go habits?" Those yearnings are still intact. In fact, as I write, she is flying home from Ohio, having visited her brother.

When the Lord returns, Mary may be among those with the most oil in their lamps, and she will have been watching for His glorious appearing!

"Even so, come, Lord Jesus!" Amen.